LEARNING TO TRUST IN FREEDOM

LEARNING TO TRUST IN FREEDOM

Signs from Jewish, Christian, and Muslim Traditions

David B. Burrell, C.S.C.

UNIVERSITY OF SCRANTON PRESS
Scranton and London

Library of Congress Cataloging-in-Publication Data

Burrell, David B.
  Learning to trust in freedom : signs from Jewish, Christian, and
Muslim traditions / David B. Burrell.
      p. cm.
  Includes bibliographical references.
  ISBN 978-1-58966-195-0 (pbk.)
  1. Philosophical theology. 2. Liberty--Religious aspects. 3. Creation-
-Comparative studies. 4. Judaism--Doctrines. 5. Islam--Doctrines. I.
Title.
  BT55.B88 2010
  202'.2--dc22

                                                          2010000889

Distribution:

UNIVERSITY OF SCRANTON PRESS
Chicago Distribution Center
11030 S. Langley
Chicago, IL 60628

PRINTED IN THE UNITED STATES OF AMERICA

CONTENTS

v

PREFACE

Time and Freedom

I BEGAN THE JOURNEY of articulating these reflections on human freedom on an Ash Wednesday, that much more grateful for the liturgical alternatives in the face of Catherine Pickstock's and Charles Taylor's reminders that modernity inevitably homogenizes time. Yet each of them punctuates that seamless homogeneity with the celebration which liturgy introduces: for Taylor, carnival preceding Ash Wednesday (offensive as it has to be to puritan and capitalist sensibilities); and for Pickstock, the way liturgical celebration can evoke virtual timelessness. Indeed, this sensibility of the "propitious" or "acceptable time" fairly constitutes what we ordinarily associate with a person's "sense of timing" or its absence. So acknowledging what is special (or "sacred") in human interactions already demands that we find ways to break with temporal homogeneity—suggesting how our lives may in fact not be pervaded by a Newtonian frame, but tend rather to be restricted to purely physical domains, much as Newtonian mechanics itself came to be relativized.

Indeed, the contrast which liturgical patterns introduce between *chronos* and *kairos* will have to be recovered in an ostensibly secular world if we are to celebrate at all! And it will be my contention that people everywhere—especially those whose lives have become enmeshed in the "tyranny of time"—are discovering that need, as a sense of something missing prompts them to seek to learn from others what they have come to find missing in their own culture. Such a realization may be reserved for the privileged, of course, as the capacity to sense something missing requires

vii

a critical stance towards one's own milieu, often triggered by dissonance or failure to achieve what has been offered as the Holy Grail. Yet all this demands that we be aware of alternatives. What we have just noted could be described as a moment of conversion, so "conversion" may offer a prescient metaphor for the authentic freedom we all seek yet which may so maddeningly elude us. Once enabled to step out of the lockstep of time, however, we may find the space within which to act freely, as many will testify by seeking time and space to reflect on a momentous decision. And it is such decisions which I want to take as paradigmatic of the freedom we hope distinguishes us as human beings, which I shall regularly contrast with simply choosing. For choosing has been so routinized and manipulated in our supermarket culture that we can easily wonder whether the choices constantly urged upon us can be said to be free at all.

When Vice-President Nixon presented Premier Khrushchev with a fully-equipped American kitchen as the epitome of freedom, the Communist leader had enough sense to respond, "Is that freedom?" And so do many of us, the more we have become enculturated to such a glittering array of choices. We may have been schooled, of course, to employ the word *choose* to range from the trivial to the portentous, yet the moment we shift from one to the other, we cannot fail to see the need to describe them differently. This inquiry into human freedom turns on recognizing that difference, and searches for ways to articulate it. Yet it may well be the case that we will find ourselves unable to locate the difference if we allow free range to the idiom of *choice*. The antidote I shall propose involves a critical scrutiny of so-called libertarian presumptions about the exercise of our freedom, only to supplement and correct them with a characteristically classical orientation to "the good."

Indeed, Aristotle long ago reminded us that while we are free to choose means to an end, the ends themselves are not up for choosing. But what could he possibly have meant, when it is *will* we are exploring, and how can we relate to the ends we pursue except by *willing* them? Here we shall find that the language of means and ends can be confusing, so some analysis will be needed, especially if we need to be persuaded that Aristotle's very distinction has any merit at all. Simply focusing on choosing can easily distract us from any consideration of the dynamics of free action, yet good novels are distinguished from trash by the way their narratives explore those very dynamics. And narrative is what we all require to ascertain how responsible our actions really are, whether they be our own or others'. This is negatively illustrated by memoirs where a reiteration of excuses obfuscates to avoid taking responsibility for actions, yet a keen ear can detect the way such evasive tactics deflect the flow of the narrative. Indeed, freedom and responsibility are correlative, since the only actions for which I can be praised or blamed are those which can be said to be my own, and it is precisely these we take to be free.

This quite natural (Aristotelian) claim shows where our account both converges and diverges from modern libertarian views, for while actions must be "my own" to be free, the precise way this action can be said to be "mine" raises concerns at once philosophical and existential. That is, we can worry whether the actions I presume to be mine are not rather determined by other forces (the philosophical issue). Or I can legitimately query whether the course of action in which I am deliberately engaged has been unduly influenced by desires of which I am only barely conscious (the existential issue). While both concerns are relevant, libertarian anxieties have focused on the philosophical issues in a quite abstract way, while our approach, dwelling as it will on the dynamics of freedom, tends to address the more existential concerns. In each case, however, the issue will be whether this action is my own, so the difference will turn on the criteria for "owning" an action.

It may be that the libertarian approach can avoid scrutinizing the dynamics of freedom because it takes agents to be autonomous individuals, fairly defined an initiators. Our critique of that presumption will question the coherence of the notion of *autonomous individual*, taking it to be a cultural construct, reflecting a certain form of social organization which cannot pretend to exhaust the *human*, and which may itself exercise hidden constraints on the very freedom it pretends to exhibit! My late colleague, Phil Quinn, remarked, "Freedom is one of the least analyzed notions I know." One reason may be that our discussion of it is laced with presumptions we have failed to assess critically, imbedded as they are in our culture—much like the air we breathe.

So this inquiry will be deliberately cross-cultural, reflecting my own work with Abrahamic faiths over the last quarter century, to allow their diverse perspectives to amplify our sense of the *humanum*, initially in the Middle Ages yet beginning to bud once again in our time.[1] In fact, it may be that the western presumption to have opened the world to a sense of freedom, in the wake of seventeenth-century religious wars and culminating in the French Revolution, may now be blocking us from seeing how those very origins have skewed our sense of freedom. Indeed, countries expressly built on that sense of freedom must explain why they have so easily allowed power to obscure their touted traditions. First tarnished by colonialism, from Ireland to Africa and Asia, and now reinforced globally by a neo-liberal economic ethos, western apologetes have mouthed the word *freedom* while effectively denying its promise to the worlds they dominate. Indeed, their actions effectively display that "the free world" requires the same indentured counterpoint as the colonialism which contributed so much to that world's development.

To complete the irony, the most consistent voices articulating this humanly disastrous situation have emanated from leaders of an institution reckoned retrograde by modern purveyors of freedom: Catholic popes from Leo XIII to John Paul II, issuing an archive of Catholic social teaching spanning over a century—from 1891 to 1991 and beyond.[2] It may be that neo-liberal blindness to these patent ironies stems from a unilateral tendency to identify freedom with "autonomous individuals," leaving its proponents blinkered regarding the socio-political consequences of such a view.[3]

Indeed, standard western philosophical treatments of freedom tend to confirm this myopia, reflecting their cultural isolation from a wider world and its aspirations, so remaining quite oblivious to the ways western myopia and denial can effectively block those very aspirations in other worlds.

By contrast, I submit that these opening reflections, dire as they are, represent an unvarnished view of the context in which we live. I pray that it is not vain to hope that what follows may help us find the heart to alter the course of things in our respective milieus, precisely by comprehending what authentic freedom might be, and then being given the inner strength to exercise it.

Acknowledgments

THESE ESSAYS OFFER a contribution to an extended inquiry exploring "Trust in Science and Religion" at Stony Brook University, under the auspices of John Templeton Foundation. Directed by Robert Crease, chair of Philosophy at Stony Brook, who assembled a core group of faculty for an ongoing seminar—and was ably assisted by James Corrigan in the manifold support such an endeavor requires—which allowed me to trace intersecting lines of trust from Jewish, Christian, and Muslim perspectives, to triangulate on a topic as pervasive as it has been unexplored. For that was the tack I was able to take, and sharing it with others brought fresh illumination each time we met. The faculty of Philosophy at Stony Brook is particularly rich and varied, a variety epitomized in the manifold interests of its chairman, Robert Crease. It is with singular joy that I offer these essays in gratitude.

A longtime colleague and friend, Jeff Gainey, offered to publish them with Scranton University Press, allowing me to share with him my indebtedness to the Templeton Foundation. "The Little Press that Could" had already published two works by Emmanuel Katongole, offering a fresh perspective on the crosscurrents of east Africa, where I am now serving my religious community, the Congregation of Holy Cross, teaching at Uganda Martyrs University. To my brothers and sisters of Holy Cross and colleagues at Uganda Martyrs I dedicate this work, helping us to explore together the reaches of freedom as desire, rather than the freedom as assertion that has devastated this region as well as West Asia.

INTRODUCTION

Freedom as Response

IF WE BEGIN WITH FREEDOM as response to "the good" rather
than as assertive initiative, we find it to be rooted in trust.
For without a native trust, we could never initiate anything.
Yet trust in Jewish, Christian, and Islamic traditions is vest-
ed in their point of fruitful intersection: the assertion that
the universe is freely created by the One. But (as Wittgenstein would ask) how can this faith-assertion gain any traction? What is it about the universe that could possibly testify to its being created? Recall that Augustine had negotiated
a harrowing inner journey before reaching the tenth book of
his *Testimony* (*Confessions*), where he was only then able to
hear things say, "We did not create ourselves."

Yet the shape of that journey already offers us a clue: a
journey through desires, it was prompted throughout by desire. So *desire* will serve as an opener; the dialectic between
desires and desire will begin to provide the traction we need
at least to wonder, for ourselves, whence things come and
wither they are going. Moreover, *desire* will lead us into
an exploration of *agency*, which offers a short answer to
the query: What is it about the universe that could possibly
testify to its being created? Nevertheless, like many such
answers, it is fraught with questions, since even the most
univocal-minded will recognize that there is no more analogous term than *act* (or *agency*), and different persons are
bound to interpret the short answer in diverse ways. So I
have chosen to follow the sinuous pathways of *desire* to offer a phenomenology of *agency* which seems at once more
faithful to our experience and may even allow a glimpse of
the expressly ineffable relation between the universe and its

creator—that is, offer some way for us to be able to perceive things as created.

To offer what Islamic thought is wont to provide—a *silsala*, or roster of those to whom one is intellectually indebted—let me mention Bernard Lonergan, my guide into philosophical theology in Rome, and René Girard, whose work I first encountered in Jerusalem some twenty-five years ago, under the mock-modest title: *Des choses cachées depuis la fondation du monde* [*Things Hidden from the Foundation of the World*]![1] I shall be citing these mentors only infrequently, yet recall them here to note how each proposes a fresh (and sometimes revolutionary) reading of the intellectual tradition in which he worked—for Lonergan, Aquinas; for Girard, Freud.

I intend to do the same, in an effort to revise conventional notions of *agency* by way of a classical typology of *desire*. Here the archetypal figure will be Plato, especially in his "erotic dialogues," the *Phaedrus* and the *Symposium*.[2] Throughout, we find the inherent correlation between *good* and *desire* structuring his work, as testified in Aristotle's axiom at the outset of his *Nichomachean Ethics* ("The good is what all things desire") together with the lapidary opening to his *Metaphysics* ("All human beings desire to know"). So the lineage between *agency* and *desire* reflects Plato, for whom "the Good" represents the source of all. Could he fasten on this language because it is inherently indeterminate, yet can also trigger a connection with action, as we know it, through *desire*?

Let us explore the fruitfulness of this classical matrix by contrasting it with current conventional notions of *action*, which, if I am not mistaken, all presume acting to be initiating. That is, the grammar of *acting* is consonant with *originating*. Yet classically, following Plato, acting originates in receiving; action is rooted in passion.[3] As another of Aristotle's lapidary summaries of Plato puts it, "Whatever is moved is moved by another"—that is, self-motion is oxymoronic; we cannot move ourselves unless something else moves us to it. (Indeed, this statement may even have been intended as a gentle correction of his mentor, for Plato had asserted that "the soul moves itself," doubtless to accentuate its unique status in the universe.)

Yet nothing could be more contrary to current conventions than to insist that self-motion is oxymoronic. Is not much of current "action theory" designed precisely to articulate self-motion over against physicalist accounts, much as libertarian accounts of human freedom strive to distinguish free action from the pervasive specter of causal determination by insisting that it is self-originating? To the extent that this is the case, I shall be offering an expressly contrary account from both Aristotle and Plato, dubbing it *classical*, with overtly anti-Hegelian overtones designed to counter a standard typology identifying classical thought as "pre-modern"—implying, of course, pre-critical, and thus easily assimilated to Kant's pejorative caricature of medieval philosophical theology as dogmatic. Yet I would contend that each intellectual epoch has engaged in critical thinking, albeit locating critical criteria differently.

On that provocative note, let us consider desire more closely, by calling to mind desires, much as Socrates will attempt to explicate the good by canvassing what we consider to be goods, only to query whether they are really good—a familiar ploy. We shall hear echoes of neo-Platonic voices, notably Plotinus, and indeed an entire panoply of such voices in Augustine. Yet these echoes will serve us well. One hardly needs be a philosopher to realize, of course, that desires are multiple and often contrary to one another. So the classical response, highlighted by neo-Platonists, was to find a set of "spiritual exercises" to allow the homing instinct of desire itself for the good to overcome its distracting multiplicity so that an overriding (or underlying) desire for the good can prevail over multiple desires for contrary goods.[4]

Notice that these philosophers never put this in terms of "control," though we will spontaneously label the exercises recommended as "ascetical practices." They are, of course, but *ascetical* invariably connotes "controlling" for us (as in "self-control"), whereas "spiritual exercises" for the ancients were more like the strategies of astute parents (or *au-pères*) who have learned to wean children from risky attractions by offering something yet more attractive to them. So *attraction*, rather than *control*, is the watchword. And herein lies a lesson: When it comes to sorting among desires, is it not more a matter of *discerning* than of *deciding*? Yet here again, we must consider how our conventional picture of deciding has been skewed as well, by a complex of presumptions which lead us to speak spontaneously of control or of will power—considering these, of course, to be actions we must initiate for them to be *our* actions.

Now, if we are correct, we would not do anything unless we wanted to—that is, unless we could construe it to be a good. Therefore, human activity is found primordially in responding more than in initiating. A few ordinary reflections should convince us that Plato and Aristotle are correct, even though a bevy of modern presumptions may keep us from recognizing these simple truths. We regularly use alarm clocks to awaken us in the morning, but unless we are able to conjure an attractive task awaiting us (or remuneration attractive enough to justify undertaking a tedious task), the snooze button is ready to hand. For while it is designed to do so, the sound of the alarm cannot "push us" out of bed; we need to be attracted to an alternative to sleep, even at so importune a moment. Similarly, once we find Jesus' recommendation to become as little children insulting to our acquired adulthood, and so renounce using the strategies of parents and *au-pères* on ourselves, we will be led to have recourse to our own will power.

Ironically, though, to the extent that we are successful in systematically exercising will power, we become even more prone to succumbing to the very desires we sought to control (by repressing them). Short of that, we become decidedly unattractive "uptight" individuals, where the watchword is indeed *individual*. Yet the persistent failure of will power to achieve control should already have alerted us to the prevailing misconception of will at work. That is, we tend to think of will as a motive power in the sense of "efficient cause," something which can push us to act. But what if willing were itself directed by a final cause, the good, so that we could (with Eleonore Stump) speak of will as "a hunger for the good"?[5] If that were the case, whatever "power" the will might be able to exercise would come not from itself but from the *good* it was pursuing. In intentional beings, final cause often trumps efficient causes; actions to which we are drawn have a better chance of being our own than those to which we are pushed.

So we may now be ready to consider cognate misconceptions of the intentional activity we associate most intimately with free action, deciding. Here the therapy required to discard our conventional notions may be even more illuminating, yet for that very reason we could find ourselves more steadfastly resisting it. Having already contrasted *discerning* with *deciding*, I shall now propose that an act of discerning rather than an assertive choosing lies at the very heart of any decision worthy of the name. It is in fact common enough to distinguish decisions from choices, reserving the term *decision* for actions more portentous than selecting among breakfast cereals on a market shelf. Yet for all that, a pervasive supermarket culture may tempt us rather to assimilate deciding to choosing, as though one actually picked one's spouse from a field of contenders. The differences which separate what I shall call "mere choosing" (as though it were a matter of simple willing, whatever that might be) from deciding are multiple and subtle, yet the chapters which follow are designed to develop strategies to assist in discriminating among them.[6]

Aristotle insists—again, contrary to conventional presumptions, and certainly counter to Jean-Paul Sartre—that we exercise choice with respect to means only, and not with respect to ends. But if we cannot be said to "choose our ends," how do we—we want to ask—"pick them"? The answer is that we don't; they rather impose themselves on us, or even better, insinuate themselves into us. For what characterizes *ends* is precisely that they are normative, so that coming to recognize that we have been pursuing the "wrong ends" will inevitably trigger a kind of conversion, for in pursuing them we have allowed them to direct (or "norm") our actions. We can always resist recognizing how wayward we have been, of course, and we call that "denial." Nor are these assertions gratuitous; they articulate what Wittgenstein calls "grammatical features" of intentional human discourse. In other words, they are stern reminders how normative our discourse already is—reminders which Lewis Carroll recalled with verve and humor in his *Through the Looking Glass*.[7]

So *discerning* seems an appropriate term to use for the way we have discriminated among the various *ends* which took over our lives at different times, and while we may be accustomed (for the reasons given) to think ourselves simply to be "choosing" one set of ends over another when we set out to "change our ways," what is at stake is more like a conversion. Moreover, using the term *conversion*, along with *discern*, to characterize the way we relate to ends, not only confirms Aristotle but also reminds us how Jean-Paul Sartre, having insisted that we can (and indeed, must) "choose our ends," was quite unable to confront the piercing query: "But how can they be normative if we simply choose them?" For whether they are right- or wrong-headed, ends are normative by their nature (to make a grammatical point).

Yet, having said all this, the conventional identification of *freedom* with *choice* is so pervasive that we may still wonder how we can say we are free unless we can do as Sartre recommended? We have seen, however, that he was doing nothing less than proposing a normative definition of freedom itself, though in doing so he violated key grammatical features of freedom as we know it. Consequently, however confused we may be about human freedom, counter-witnesses such as Sartre can remind us that we already know something about it, touching on its very grammar. So then, to return to our current query: If deciding is more than simply choosing, what makes it to be more? Can we describe that feature more clearly?

I believe we have assembled the materials to do so. For just as language usage can help us discriminate among diverse feelings, attitudes, or orientations, so our attempts to describe such things will come up against inbuilt grammatical structures, and so the practice acquired by discriminating among ends can bring us to recognize that one course of action is preferable to another—and by a certain inevitability. Consider the following linguistic clue regarding the discernment at play in deciding. No language other than American English speaks of "*making* a decision." British English follows the pattern of romance languages in "*taking* a decision," while Germans may even use the expression "*meeting* a decision." Now "taking a decision" is closer to receiving it, and so leads us into the logical neighborhood of discerning, rather than merely choosing.

Indeed, this must be what Aristotle was gesturing towards in insisting that we choose means, but not ends. And if our phenomenology has been persuasive enough to begin to deconstruct standing presumptions about free action, we will not only have vindicated the use of classical strategies to expose the weakness endemic to current discourse about these matters. We will have also prepared ourselves to examine the assertions of Jewish, Muslim, and Christian traditions to see how faith in a free creator might help us reach a more positive characterization of freedom, one rooted in trust rather than self-assertion. And as we do so, we shall try as well to show how such a conception of freedom is more congruent with our experience than prevailing libertarian accounts.

CHAPTER ONE

Learning from Traditions to Overcome
the Pastness of the Past:
From Modernity to Postmodernity

CURRENT PHILOSOPHICAL TREATMENTS of freedom prove to be remarkably thin, content to demonstrate that there is such a thing in the face of the bugbear of determinism.[1] Moreover, the thing in question is identified with "the ability to do otherwise," a formula which proves to be quite unstable in the face of actual practice, as Eleonore Stump's maternal counter-examples display.[2] What seems unaccountably missing is any sustained description of the dynamics of free action. Yet that is precisely what Aquinas supplies, as Eleonore Stump has so clearly tracked in her book entitled *Aquinas*. Why such insouciance for the details in standard philosophical accounts? Anxieties about determinism may go a long way towards explaining a blindness to other features of freedom, but once that bugbear has been set aside, why rest content with the thin and contentious "ability to do otherwise"? Surely human freedom holds more promise than that.

My admittedly speculative diagnosis may appear to carry us far afield, but could also prove useful in identifying some presumptions that help render us myopic to the issues involved in human freedom. For it is my contention that as neo-Thomistic philosophy was unwittingly truncated by regarding the natural/supernatural distinction more like a divide, so modern and contemporary philosophy felt compelled to account for humanity without reference to a transcendent goal, by attempting to speak of creatures without reference to a creator.

1

Ironically, we shall see how standard analyses of a libertarian cast foster a dualistic picture, whereas Aquinas's account (replete with a creator) offers a holistic account of human freedom. The difficulty does not rest with what distinguishes libertarian analyses from their alternatives: in the jargon, "compatibilist" or even "hard determinist." But, for strategic reasons, my critique will focus on philosophers who adopt libertarian analyses while averring creation. Indeed, I shall contend that their unwitting adoption of categories constructed to avoid reference to a creator can prevent them from seeing how crucial that omission can be. The ensuing scheme may help to identify references to a creator.

Years teaching a course in ancient and medieval philosophy have led me to identify the difference between the two quite clearly: that is, the difference between the presence or the absence of a free creator. Jewish, Christian, and Muslim thinkers converged in their efforts to insert a free creator into the apparently seamless Hellenic philosophy they inherited.[3] (Josef Pieper's observation that "creation is the hidden element in the philosophy of St. Thomas" alerted many of us to this operative difference from Aristotle, one many Thomists have regularly managed to overlook in their anxiety to mark a divide between philosophy and theology.)[4] Yet if we can say, schematically, that the presence of a free creator divides medieval from ancient philosophy, what marks the subsequent transition to modern philosophy? Many cultural shifts, no doubt, but to continue speaking schematically, modern philosophy wanted to distinguish itself by eliminating theological overtones present in "scholastics," so proceeded by avoiding reference to a creator. [5]

The creator was a bit large to overlook, however, so the gradual tendency was to deny its relevance, as evidenced in Enlightenment fascination with "the Greeks." The reference is more constructed than historical, though Aristotle, after all, had managed quite well without a creator. Now if that be the case (again, speaking quite schematically) we can characterize modern philosophy as "post-medieval," with the *post-* prefix carrying a note of denial—in this case, of a creator, either directly or implicitly. A cursory look at the strategies whereby modern philosophers compensated for the absence of a creator, however, shows them to lead inescapably to foundational grounds such as "self-evident" propositions or "sense data." When these prove illusory, we cannot but enter a postmodern world.

Nevertheless, if our understanding of philosophy itself (à la Rorty) is inherently linked to such strategies, then we will inevitably regard a postmodern context as one in which "anything goes," since we are now bereft of the "foundations" which did duty for a creator. Here is where our scheme can help. If modern philosophy can be seen as "post-medieval," then postmodern philosophy will have to be read as "post post-medieval." And while the *post-* prefixes may not connote the same sort of denials, the double "negations" direct us to a sense of postmodern which bears affinities with medieval inquiry. Put more positively and less schematically, both medieval and postmodern inquiries are more at ease with Gadamer's contention that every inquiry rests on fiduciary premises.[6] In practice, this means that faith may be regarded as integral to knowing, though (like any other contribution to knowing) it will always be subject to critical interpretation. So Descartes' stark division between faith and knowing becomes passé.

This scheme can help us to see three things: (1) Gadamer's contention about all inquiry resting on fiduciary premises, already anticipated by Newman's *Grammar of Assent*,[7] can lead us to a constructive reading of the inescapably postmodern world into which we have been thrust, (2) such fiduciary premises will have to be tested themselves, so the hermeneutics developed in theological arenas may prove useful to philosophical inquiry, and (3) presuppositions extant in modern inquiries may prove misleading in a world which has "lost faith in reason"—a contention which would be oxymoronic to Descartes, yet is perfectly understandable when the "reason" in question is presumed to be a "pure reason" absent all presuppositions.

Armed with these strategies, we can proceed to my contentious thesis: currently standard accounts of freedom (focused on libertarian freedom) will prove radically inadequate to parsing the nuances and complexities of human freedom and will lead to anti-theological conclusions, precisely because the analytic categories such accounts presume have been developed in an intellectual atmosphere inattentive to the presence of a creator—or indeed of any significant finality to the *humanum*. Ironically, one can find "theists" espousing such accounts, quite unaware of the way the categories they employ insist on the absence of a creator.

Finally—as if this were not enough—such truncated accounts of freedom will prove unable to counter the corrosively postmodern contention that "all is power," since the way in which they identify freedom with choosing, so as to eschew any *telos* inherent to free actions, allows freedom to be rendered as "doing what I wanna do." As a result, gratification and domination quickly fill the void in an account which had neglected the dynamics of desire from the outset.

I shall illustrate this complex thesis with salient examples from customary practices of dominating groups (such as Israeli settlers) to show how such accounts of freedom license corruption by motives of power, lightly masked with ideological justification. Ironically, once freedom is simply identified with choosing, as in the slogan "pro-choice," there is little to keep it from being exercised coercively on others. Once the *telos* inherent to free action has been explicitly eschewed, the way lies open to unabashedly use our freedom to promote our own gratification. If that describes the policies of the hefty actors on our world stage, then we may have traced a path to one of the intellectual supports for this pervasive evil.

Free Action as Initiative or Response?

Perhaps the most telling insight into the skewed dynamics of libertarian freedom occurs in a 1964 lecture by Roderick Chisholm; citing Aristotle, he insists that the will must be a prime mover.[8] Examining the reference to Aristotle will help correct his contention, however, for he takes Aristotle's prime mover to be an initiator—a "pusher," if you will—whereas Aristotle's own reasoning requires that it be unmoved, so as to move whatever moves by being the object of its desire. In short, Aristotle's account of movement incorporates Plato's accent on the good by postulating a world of essences each intent on a proper end, and all drawn, in an orderly fashion, to the good itself. But in a world bereft of teleology, a prime mover would have to initiate, as Chisholm presumed. What else could establish its primacy in moving? But while the dynamic scheme from Plato through Aristotle to Aquinas offered a coherent account of action as a response to a proper good, simply postulating an initiating power offers no account at all. Whence this mysterious power?

Here we see the temptation to a form of dualism: one must postulate a power of a special sort, operating within, yet independent of, the world of nature, to account for the presence of such prime movers with their innate power to initiate. Moreover, the tendency of this account to eschew any further articulation of the dynamics of free action will also make one wonder why one path is chosen rather than another. In short, there seems a direct lineage from early forms of "voluntarism" to libertarian accounts of freedom, for any query why one chose one direction in preference to another will have to invoke teleology—and teleology shifts our focus to the end in view. Put simply, does one push oneself out of bed in the morning, or is one rather drawn by the prospect of something enticing? Anything else, like punishment for being late for work, would threaten the freedom of one's rising. Moreover, to acknowledge that there may always be a little of both retains the focus on the goal, whether it be more compelling or more enticing.

So if the classical scheme simply makes more sense—is phenomenologically more compelling, if you will—why is it so conspicuously absent from current accounts of freedom? And why are those who give such accounts not embarrassed by their inability to depict the dynamics of free action? My contention is that these accounts have been schooled to avoid any reference to an orderly universe so as to pretend to focus on the action of individuals. Yet individuals respond to situations, so are already imbedded in linguistic (as well as pre-linguistic) patterns of response. Once we are reminded of this, as we are, so effectively, by Alasdair MacIntyre,[9] then his contention that "the individual" is an eighteenth-century abstraction begins to ring true.

Alternately, as Eleonore Stump has developed so clearly (and Mary Clark had sketched before her), the subtle interactions of intellect and will delineated by Aquinas offer a promising path for displaying the dynamics of human freedom.[10] Moreover, a classical account readily explains the indeterminacy of freedom, which moderns seem to value as its very core, for an inherent orientation to "the good" can never settle the best way to attain it. And the same architectonic scheme also allows for a moment in free action which even radicalizes the celebrated "ability to do otherwise," in that each of us retains the ability to reject the dynamic itself, and so perform actions that are evil.

Here too, the classical scheme offers a more phenomenologically satisfying analysis, since good and evil do not appear as simple contraries, as though one could as readily choose one or the other as alterative options. Indeed, the very grammar of evil demands that we first acknowledge the primacy of good, otherwise there would be no evil, but only an alternate way of acting. On this account, an evil act is less of an act, illustrated at its limit by a person caught in the downward spiral of addiction—who can hardly be said to be acting in a full-blooded sense. So while rejecting the dynamic itself may offer a manifest case of our being "able to do otherwise," rejection can hardly be considered paradigmatic for free action, since acts flowing from such a refusal are manifestly deficient as acts.[11]

Finally, any account that would make human beings mere "choice machines" must overlook the goal-directedness of human development. Yet the caricature is clearly just that, whereas acts of choosing are always imbedded in a rich texture of desires, so it is attention to desire which most recommends the classical account of freedom. For ironically, by eschewing reference to desire, a standard account— particularly a "thin" libertarian one—leaves our choices at their mercy. Failing to advert to the dynamics of our desires simply invites self-deception regarding the freedom of our actions, since "what we wanna do" seldom originates from our very selves, and is usually elicited by multiple (and often powerfully presented) enticements, to which we are ever vulnerable.

Indeed, when we contrast Platonic (and later, Augustinian) depictions of the tyranny of desire with accounts which focus on "the ability to do otherwise," the latter is manifestly limp, notably from failing to attend to desires. Moreover, desire roots our actions in the world of nature in which we partake, thus heading off dualist temptations. But given the ubiquity of desire, where then does our freedom lie? It lies in assenting or not to such desires, of course, but doing so in a way which orders the myriad desires in a discerning manner; not mere (and usually nugatory) willpower.

In fact, were we able to muster it, to what end would such power be directed? Here the classical scheme can be enriched with a creator, who names and personifies Plato's good. And that creator, as Aquinas insists, will be present in all authentically free actions—absent only from those which deny the orientation inherent to our intellect and will, and even then only from the orientation itself.[12] For every action qua action will be a created action, though what makes an action evil—its departure from the orientation to the good sketched above—will come from the creature alone, as it exercises its power to disconnect from its creator in acting. (But, more on this later.)

From Freedom as Assertion to Raw Assertion of Power, with Some Powerful Antidotes

When freedom is celebrated as the sheer power to initiate action, or identified with choosing, it cannot help becoming in practice "doing what I wanna do," yet that scheme leaves no room to appreciate or to assess the power of our wants. So the Promethean image of control, with its cognate willpower, dominates. Yet when agents lack such control, as we often do, some authority will be required to constrain them, the most interior of these constraints being the imperatives of practical reason, reinforced for believers by divine commands.

So, once one's account of free actions no longer requires a creator to empower them, God re-enters as the one who constrains this unlimited freedom by divine legislation. As a consequence, contrary to Paul as well as to Luther, law becomes the centerpiece of Puritan Christianity. But as Nathaniel Hawthorne and others have poignantly reminded us, however internal such constraints were meant to be for believers, they remain external to the Promethean picture of freedom they were intended to constrain; they can only hope to succeed in constraining freedom of action in a social order as efficacious as Puritan society.

The minimal characterization of freedom as "the ability to do otherwise" deprives human freedom of any internal structure, stripping it of any inherent constraints. When the constraining social order collapses, as social orders tend to do—especially when undermined by a notion of freedom as "doing what I wanna do"—individuals emerge, constrained only by Kant's formal imperatives or those of revelation (or, in practice, a combination of both). Ultimately, as we shall see, since even these (purportedly interior) constraints remain external to the (unarticulated) dynamic of free action, they can easily be manipulated to serve one's progress to gratification.

Doubtless many cultural and economic factors conspired to create the resulting "individual," but the view of freedom which has prevailed will help to assure that the life and liberty such individuals stoutly defend will be—in function of the happiness they are intent on pursuing—focused on individual gratification, for this scheme of freedom offers no further resources. Lacking an inherent *telos*, we have no way of asking what freedoms are for.[13] All this conveniently serves that picture of society called political liberalism, of course, yet the inescapable logic of gratification assures that such liberals will, before long, become political libertarians, as care for the common good gives way to economic power, reducing any touted republic to an oligarchy, mocking the "soft" constraints of civil rights and international law in the name of "interests"—usually financially defined.

Can we any longer doubt this to be the outcome, or at least the inevitable concomitant, of a libertarian analysis of freedom? But we are asked, "What is the alternative?" as our interlocutors fear a return to the repressions of Puritan society. Let us explore an alternative, that of Augustine, in the following chapter.

CHAPTER TWO

Contrasting Acting as Initiating with Acting as Responding:
A Classical View of Will

LET US BEGIN BY TRACING the sinuous path whereby free action became detached from desire. Kant's crucial dictum—"Only the will can be good"—best initiates this brief aetiology explaining how *will* became separated from *desire*; it is brief, since the story has often been recounted.[1] For Kant, we recall, the separation was a strategic one: desire was part of nature, so the will which makes agents to be free had to be part of the noumenal world, operating within, yet independent of, the world of nature. Yet Kant's separation is rooted in Scotus's bifurcation of will from intellect, a strategy apparently executed in response to the famous condemnations of 1277.[2] (We shall see that while Aquinas spoke of intellect and of will as distinct, they are intimately interconnected for him.) So the agent for Scotus is the will, counseled, so to say, by the intellect. Yet what makes one move is the will's so-called *actus elicitus*.[3]

The resulting primacy of the will served Scotus's Franciscan roots as well. Although Kant's concerns, notably his epistemological strategies, were quite different, will also became crucial for him—to allow human beings access to realities which lie beyond the scientific knowledge appropriate to them. Yet the will in question had already been isolated by Scotus, with the inevitable result: commands—in Kant's language, imperatives—rather than intellectual discernment, would govern its activity. (The so-called divine command theory of ethics originates in this strategy.) Moreover, desires (as part of nature) become irrelevant to

11

moral decision, often clouding and hindering an authentically ethical stance. The resulting puritan picture is evident in the center of hell: the very antithesis of happiness, for Milton, a raging fire stoked by wayward desires—in stark contrast to Dante's classical picture, a block of ice, the utter absence of desire.

We shall develop, with Augustine's help, the role which desire plays in the classical dynamics of intellect and will, yet for now there is one more salient step. Such a will, one that is sovereign, best exercises itself in controlling one's life—notably, of course, one's desires; *control* becomes the key term. *Control* suggests *willpower*, which then allows us to ask this question: Does the will control me, or do I control my will? The question is endemic, of course, to any faculty account. Is it my intellect which knows, or do I know in virtue of my intellect? The coherent answer has to be that it is the subject who knows or wills, of course, though the mode of discourse which Scotus introduced of a detached will tends to make the question quite intractable here. However that is resolved, it is the preoccupation with control which attends our analysis. For with control comes independence, the distinguishing feature of free action in this model.

Here, matters take a theological turn, as exhibited in standard forms of the "free will" defense attending the "problem of evil." If human freedom is to be the source of evil (as Augustine insisted), then this strategy demands that human free actions be utterly free, that is, bereft of any divine influence. If those who have promoted this strategy had been alert to precedents in the history of philosophy, they would have recognized the lineaments of the early Islamic Mu'tazilites, similarly intent on preserving "divine justice" along with the autonomy of human freedom.[4] The crucial step lies in removing free human actions from divine sovereignty, with the premise—explicit for Muslims, yet normally implicit for our contemporaries—that any authentic action must be regarded as a creation ex nihilo. Even though the creator must be understood to create everything, this strategy neatly exempts human actions from that universal set: human beings alone create their actions, else they could hardly be said to be free.

While political influences soon began to undermine this teaching in early Islam, inherent factors were at work as well. If Islam divides the creator from everything else, exempting human actions from the creator's sovereignty removes a considerable slice of the created universe from creation itself! So orthodox Islam soon adopted a subtle strategy whereby God creates what we perform, reserving responsibility to humans for their actions, good or evil, while respecting divine sovereignty.[5]

This is not so for many of our contemporaries, however, largely because their discourse also remains remarkably unsophisticated regarding the founding activity of creation and the resultant unique relation of creatures to their creator.[6] Lacking a coherent picture of creation as the unique causal activity it must be, the creator will inevitably be regarded as another operator in the scene—and as a rival to created agency. The result must then be to withdraw free human actions from the created realm, as oxymoronic as that sounds and is.

The effect is even worse, however, since the resultant "creator" can no longer be the God whom Jews, Christians, and Muslims worship, but can only be "the biggest thing around."[7] Thus failing to attempt a proper articulation of the act of creation effectively sidelines proper consideration of the unique relation which distinguishes creator from creatures—and, at the same time, unites them.[8]

While there is neither time nor space to elaborate this here, it should suffice to note how others, notably Aquinas, had recourse to Neo-Platonic strategies to articulate the creator as "cause of being."[9] This strategy will require a robust understanding of being as act, however, to which Aquinas was able to give philosophical voice by transforming Avicenna's celebrated distinction between being and essence.[10] The result is a rich scenario of the universe participating in being as it emanates from a creator. Here a great deal of work has been done to clarify Plato's original notion of participation, which Aristotle had criticized as a "mere metaphor."[11] Yet even these sophisticated accounts may still appear to be so much metaphor to those who fail to struggle with the way in which creating a universe must exceed any understanding of causation which we regularly employ—as Kant saw so well.

Once a creator emerges on the scene, it appears that we cannot have a proper grasp of human·freedom without imbedding it in that created order. Indeed, unless we do this quite explicitly, the restored creator will inevitably be regarded as the largest item in the universe, and, consequently, a threat to human freedom. The effect of failing to clarify the unique founding activity of creation can only leave self-styled "theists" one exit strategy: remove human free action from the creator's ambit, thereby undermining the original avowal of the Abrahamic faiths of a free sovereign creator of the universe.

To return to our orienting scheme relating classical to medieval, modern, and postmodern presumptions for philosophical inquiry, it seems that the imposing presence of a creator impedes a simple return to the classical picture of human beings oriented to the good. As Kierkegaard has suggested, that picture may now appear too naive, or perhaps the very introduction of a creator can lead to imagining human agents as creators in their own right, as it were.[12] Yet both Bible and Qur'an warn us that adopting that image for ourselves will lead to unimaginable evil. To be "like god" is tantamount to refusing the original covenant whereby human beings vow their obedience to the Lord of all.[13] What results, of course, is the human world in which we all live, which Aquinas neatly distinguished from the world of nature which God creates by noting how "evil for the most part prevails" in the world which human beings have made.[14]

Can we early twenty-first-century people gainsay that radical observation? Yet it may help us to trace the path from a metaphysics which asserts free action to be an unexplained initiative to a rudderless view of freedom which can no longer ask what freedoms are for, so leading ineluctably to a general insouciance about domination of the rich and powerful. We shall try to relieve the bleakness of this analysis by presenting comparative views of contrasting alternatives.

Invoking the Guidance of Augustine

The alternative I shall try to elaborate takes its bearings from Augustine's analysis of wants and desires, especially as they conspire to form communities of discourse and of action. Such communities could offer striking witness to a society inspired by the vision of freedom outlined here. Commenting on the first letter of John promising that "we shall be like him, for we shall see him as he is" (John 3.2), Augustine presents "the entire life of a good Christian [as] an exercise of holy desire. You do not see what you long for, but the very act of desiring prepares you, so that when he comes you may see and be utterly satisfied." Sometimes, he says, we find that we need to stretch a sack or wineskin to accommodate an extraordinary amount: "This is how God deals with us. Simply by making us wait, he increases our desire, which in turn enlarges the capacity of our soul, making it able to receive what is to be given to us. So, my brethren, continue to desire, for we shall be filled. [Yet] this exercise will be effective only to the extent that we free ourselves from desires leading to infatuation with this world."[15] We find ourselves to be a battleground of desires, yet it is desire itself which will lead us to victory— though not as our achievement, but as a gift. He presumes that our orientation to the good represents an endowment from the creator—itself an original gift, which when followed on its own terms, will be crowned with the supreme gift: to become like that very creator. So all is gift, which we will be enlarged to receive once we free ourselves from infatuations leading (as Paul said) to death.

The gift of the promise, together with the gift promised, entails a task defining the context and the point of our freedom: to return everything to the One from whom we have received everything. A task of that sort will take nothing short of a lifetime to accomplish, but it can be accomplished little by little, through discrete actions embodying that very orientation. The image is progressive; as infatuations are sloughed off, noble desires are in part realized and the true self begins to emerge. Indeed, on this account there can be no definition of *true self* other than one completely open to receiving the gift of this promise: to be assimilated to the One whose gift of being constitutes our very existence. This is all very heady stuff, nor does Augustine expect us to understand the words; it is rather our desires that will show us the proper way as we learn to discriminate among them, following those that lead to life and renouncing those leading to death.[16]

Will, for Augustine (as well as Aquinas), is suffused with desire and discernment, which together will lead us to our true self as we follow the orientation with which we are endowed at creation, bolstered by "an anointing by the Holy One which teaches us inwardly more than our tongue can speak."[17] In his *Confessions*, he details the dialectic of desire in his own case, tracing his journey through multiple infatuations to the point where he allowed the guiding desire to fill his soul and take over the direction of his life: "The light of confidence flooded into my heart."[18]

This account of freedom differs notably from standard analyses in that a free act becomes a response rather than an initiative, as one accepts the invitation to fulfill the original orientation. The freedom it offers is progressive as well: actions become more authentically one's own, and hence more integrally free, to the extent that one is freed from the hold of infatuations to follow those desires which contribute to fulfilling the orienting desire. So all is gift, and all is desire, while desires properly discerned lead to a freedom liberated from infatuations—*non est liber nisi liberatus*, "no one is free until freed." We are as far from an off/on exercise of freedom as we are from an off/on picture of existence.[19]

It is the orientation to the creator built into our very existing which empowers this activity of responding, so that, far from being a hindrance, a proper appreciation of the creator/creature relationship actually enables created freedom—now positively characterized as a return to one's source rather than a pointless assertion of a posited power. The exercise of freedom then offers a path to the true self, however sinuous and twisting its route may be. Alternately, allowing oneself to be caught in the tangle of infatuations will divert one from one's true self, so such a random array of choices will in fact be deficient as an exercise of freedom, stemming as it does from refusing rather than accepting the gift. While we are uncannily skilled in keeping this deficiency from becoming manifest, this account presumes that it will tend to become so, since staving off the demands of the orienting desire will come to prove awkward. That is indeed the hope, as well as offering grounds for hope, even though the radical reach of this freedom can also extend to the very loss of self, as one rejects the gift by refusing the orientation. Yet this account avoids elevating that refusal into the paradigm of freedom itself, thereby confirming a rich vein of contemporary literature which suggests that an account which rejects a creator with its grounding orientation may lead ineluctably to loss of self.

A libertarian account of freedom need not of itself lead to such a self-defeating end. By deliberately eschewing offering a point to the exercise of freedom, it can introduce a pointlessness which opens the gates to gratification masked as freedom. (Recall how Augustine's "pear tree incident" introduces pointlessness as the core of evil.) The dynamics are quite simple. If freedom amounts to choosing, and my choices are directed by and to what I want, then allowing my wants free reign invites harnessing my intellectual powers to justifying what I *want* to do, rather than to discerning what I *ought* to do.

Moreover, if oughts are Kantian-wise opposed to wants, then personal and collective experience shows which will win. Our resourcefulness at finding justifications is only matched by our virtuosity for making excuses, so "will as want" inevitably prevails. Levinas had hoped that the very presence of the "other," notably of another person, would confront our endemic inertial tendency to gratification, thereby lifting us to an ethical plane not unlike that envisaged by Kant. But collectives seem able to obscure even this dynamic by the handy ruse of demonization. A messianic cadre of West Bank settlers no longer sees Palestinians as fellow human beings, but as obstacles to completing the settlement of a land that is exclusively theirs by divine right. While their gratuitous acts of expropriation and humiliation appear manifestly inhuman to onlookers, any call to regard their Palestinian neighbors as neighbors asks them to reject an entire justificatory scheme.

The ease with which that scheme can obscure what we (and Levinas) take to be simple human decency is certainly facilitated by an account of freedom bereft of any inherent goals, so rendering all constraints external to itself. But if that be the case, it suggests that "simple human decency" will require a richer view of human freedom to make its demands felt. It may well be that something like the normative account which we have offered, replete with a creator to empower its direction and execution, comes far closer to the kind of freedom we need to be human and decent. The alternative, attempting to avoid so potent a metaphysics by simply equating freedom with choosing, leads rather to an illusory freedom whereby we effectively become prey to wayward desires.

CHAPTER THREE

Creation and Cosmic Trust in Abrahamic Faith Traditions

WE MIGHT BE WELL SERVED to regard Jewish, Christian, and Islamic traditions as their respective medieval intellectual representatives did, as fulfilling Plato's overriding focus on the Good, now given a name. That name was, however, was unpronounceable among the Jews, pronounced by Jesus only by adopting the colloquial *Abba* ("Father," which he invited his followers to use), and immediately expanded into ninety-nine variants in Islam. Now, names name individuals, yet the medieval thinkers from these three traditions—Maimonides, Aquinas, al-Ghazali—concurred in insisting that this One is not an individual being. Being an individual, in our terms, would inhibit displaying that the One is creator of all that is. But once the focus has been directed to a personal One, as the genres of Jewish, Christian, and Muslim scriptures suggest, the same intentional focus will also be required if the creator is to act freely in creating all that is.

Insisting that creation be free may go beyond the letter of the scriptures, whose accounts (befitting any discourse about the origination of all that is) were sketchy at best. Nevertheless, highlighting the originating act as free serves to condense the multivalent meaning of those same scriptures to a basic message: the creator could have no other motive than largesse in bringing creatures into being, lest the One be beholden to anything else and so act out of need. The very notion of creator for Jews, Christians, and Muslims demands that creating be a free act.

19

Establishing that fact required a great deal of philosophical sophistication at the time, however, given the preponderance of emanation theories elaborated to give coherent accounts of the origin of the universe from the One (Plotinus).[1] Yet the shift to a personal focus carried cognate difficulties as well. (Could not such a One simply act willfully?) By contrast with Plotinus's intellectual austerity, does not bringing origination to a personal focus invite a return of the very anthropomorphism which Plotinus had sought to purify? Each of the respective scriptures, as we might suspect, has ways of offsetting such misreadings of a personal One, reinforced by the ensuing traditions. In the Hebrew scriptures, the book of Job stands out, for it obviously intends to counter a "mechanical" way of reading the covenant presented in Deuteronomy—whereby those who reject the promise, with its responsibilities, will be punished, while those who follow it will be rewarded. Job directs his address to the very source of the covenant, bypassing abstract conceptions of justice by appealing to the inscrutable One, and in the end is praised for "having spoken well of me" by the same heavenly voice which condemns the pretence of his companions to know the ways of God.[2]

So these three traditions concur in insisting that we cannot adequately articulate the relation between the One and all that is, though we must affirm that it is personal. The relation will remain ineffable because our creaturely perspectives keep us from speaking coherently of the provenance of all that is, except to insist that it be free and thus personal in character, which we only learn from revelation. Indeed, precisely in as much as Hebrew scriptures and the Qur'an speak of a covenantal "interaction" between this One and the people so covenanted, the abiding source of the relationship remains with God, thereby supplying the corrective that is specific in the book of Job. Any attempt to "justify the ways of God" to human beings (theodicy) must remain otiose, unless one is speaking of a "supreme being" in philosophical categories quite oblivious of the nuances of these traditions of revelation.

Yet what do I accomplish by bringing Plato's primacy of the Good to a personal focus? How can I clam that it fulfills Plato? What would it mean to do that?

Let us employ the book of Job to show how the fresh perspective offered by the Abrahamic faiths can effectively release human freedom, precisely by facilitating a personal relationship on the part of intentional creatures with this inscrutable and ineffable—yet personal—One. Although that relationship will have to be shaped and informed by astute philosophical reflection, to counteract the incoherencies inevitable when operating within this ineffable relation, the relationship itself must be immediate, as creating is an immediate act of the creator. When it can be sustained, such a relationship will be an unfailing source of trust, grounded as it is in a cosmic trust—that trust which the Qur'an (33:72, 7:172) has the creator extending to humankind "in the beginning," thus animating a personal relation in those who are as aware as humans can be of that grounding source.

Though articulating this rapport is professedly difficult, we could express it colloquially by acknowledging how believing the universe to be freely created by the One is a preposterous thing to believe, yet noting that those who do so have at least the chance of seeing their lives as a vocation, while those bereft of such an a abiding personal source can at best struggle with a career. An astute philosopher, John Searle, himself an outspoken advocate of intentionality in opposition to materialist accounts of human beings, gave indirect testimony to the potency of this distinction (in a personal exchange at a conference) when he found himself unable to recognize any difference between *vocation* and *career*.

Yet it may be that philosophers who are tone-deaf to my contention could offer indirect testimony to its validity, suggesting how a life lived in this personal focus can open fresh perspectives on the universe and our mode of being within it, while the very distinction which emerges as crucial could easily escape one bereft of that personal relation. Moreover, such indirect ways of knowing will tend to be the case in these matters, so we can only hope that personal witness might prompt others to wonder whether there is not more to heaven and earth than can be found in one's philosophy.[3]

Some of the current debates on "science and religion" exhibit a similar tone-deafness for something more, as Terry Eagleton has effectively limned.[4] Might we identify this something more as a kind of cosmic trust which enlivens all of our inquiry and each of our relationships?[5] Local communities of trust are quite possible, it seems, without being explicitly grounded in such a cosmic trust, yet they inevitably remain vulnerable to shifting priorities among their participants, to say nothing of fatigue engendered by keeping them going, especially in the counter-cultural mode which they must inevitably espouse.[6]

Indeed, trust itself is counter-cultural, as is hope. Hope, when it does emerge, does so from the ashes of optimism—so trust can surface only when naive confidence can no longer be sustained. How and why hope or trust emerges, however, can escape us. These reflections have so far utilized the dialectic of desire, via desires, to show the way to a converging narrative of origin for both hope and trust. Yet were that narrative to lead us to the cusp of an interpersonal encounter with the origin of hope and trust, the ensuing encounter would offer a way to transform standard philosophical accounts of human freedom by exhibiting a dramatic shift from freedom as initiating to freedom as responding.

That, I suggest, is the enduring message of the book of Job. Offered ostensibly as a corrective to recurring impersonal distortions of a revelation thoroughly personal at root, the poetic author executes his task by restoring that original context through an interpersonal encounter. For Job's "friends" had sought to divert his torment by offering explanations, while he retained his dignity and displayed his freedom by appealing directly to the source of his torment—and of his freedom. They spoke about God while Job spoke to his God, thereby unveiling the object of *their* discourse to be an idol—in stark contrast to the subject to whom Job directly addresses his plaintive pleas, and from whom he receives an equally direct response. The result is distinctively postmodern.

While modernity sought to supplant theological reflection with philosophical clarification, replacing narratives with theories, one of the features which renders postmodernity "post-" is its tendency towards nonreduction, towards reconciling diverse modes of discourse in the interest of understanding what each mode seeks to express. Admittedly, this is a benign postmodernity, akin to that of John Henry Newman, Bernard Lonergan, or even (at times) John Paul II. The story of Job can help us see that what makes theirs benign is precisely its grounding in scripture.

Scriptures can leave ambiguous legacies, however, as Jews and Christians (with Muslims) know so well, one of which the book of Job seeks explicitly to correct in the Hebrew scriptures. Moreover, in showing how this critical biblical poet accomplishes that, we can also observe how the very structure of the book can be employed to deconstruct theories, notably theodicies which had aspired to disambiguate the scriptures even better than scripture itself attempted in the book of Job.

There is no doubt, however, that the very narrative framing Job's story—a divinity bargaining with its alter ego, Satan, sets up a quasi-philosophical problematic, inviting modernist redaction. But placing that framing conceit in the larger scriptural context which the entire book presumes, while trenchantly criticizing a narrow appropriation of it, should remind us how God-soaked that context is. Indeed, the book itself emanates a ray of hope, finding its way through multiple baffle-plates like the sun illuminating the headstone at Newgrange at its winter solstice. Nevertheless, while a prima facie reading of the story framing the book of Job may suggest a classical theodicy of divine testing as well as of reward and punishment, attending to the structure of the book can help us see just how misguided a reading that is. Indeed, an unencumbered reading of the book readily shows how the unfolding drama—notably in

the counterpoint between each of Job's friends and Job himself—belies such an interpretation.

While Job's friends each address arguments to Job regarding God's supposed yet hidden plans, his riposte to
their arguments is addressed not to them but to the over-
whelming presence of the God of Israel in a dialogue quite
implicit throughout. In the end, the reality of that dialogue
is confirmed by that very God, as the One signs off by an-
nouncing His preference for Job above all of the rest, who
rather incur the wrath of that God for attempting to defend
His ways! Recalling that this is the very One who has tak-
en such care to reveal His ways to a particular people (to
whom Job does not belong), we cannot escape concluding
that the entire dramatic exchange—between Job and his interlocutors, and even more between Job and the God of Israel—must be directed against a recurrent misappropriation
of that revelation on the part of the people entrusted with
it. So it must be that the book's primary role in the Hebrew
canon is to correct that endemic misapprehension of biblical
revelation displayed by Job's friends, as their explanation of
his plight turns on taking the covenant to be a set of impersonal transactions. They insist that good things are in store
for all who abide by the Torah while affliction attends anyone who does not, leading them to infer that Job must have
transgressed God's command, for he is afflicted.

Indeed, as his friends have appropriated the covenant,
wrongdoing is at once a necessary and a sufficient condition
for affliction as a form of punishment, much as a felicitous
life is logically linked to observance of the right way. Yet it
is telling that Job himself seems not to have internalized the
simple scheme which his friends both presume and represent, the terms of which seem to be set by the framing story. (Could *that* be why the creator presents him to Satan as
truly just?) Yet the double bind into which they try to press
Job is anything but ironic: admit your wrongdoing and re-
pent! In the terms framing the story itself, such an admis-
sion would constitute a self-serving prevarication, not unlike those "confessions" elicited by Soviet show trials. So

we find Herbert Fingarette identifying this legal dilemma as the authentic dramatic frame of the book: Job could only release himself from the bind which his friends create by perjuring himself.[7]

The dramatic context is an explicitly legal one, as Job himself expresses in contending with the God of Israel. Yet Job's conduct of his own defense will also serve to deconstruct that legal context, to culminate in an encounter with that One whom the Hebrew scriptures credit with establishing the context itself. More directly, if the God in question is pictured throughout as judge, we find Job less interested in what any judge may think of his defense (in the face of his prosecuting friends) than he is in appealing directly to the creator-judge himself: "Only grant two things to me, then I will not hide myself from your face: withdraw your hand from me, and do not let dread of you terrify me. Then call, and I will answer; or let me speak, and you reply to me" (Job 13:20–22).

Rather than treat the creator as a judge who must adjudicate by the rules, Job appeals directly to the creator as the One who sets the very rules under which Job has been told he must consider his affliction as punishment, so effectively transmuting this One into an interlocutor. Moreover, the legal frame gives Job no other choice, for to accept the rules as detailed by his friends would demand that he perjure himself, expressly engaging in the very wrongdoing which he has so far consciously avoided.

Nevertheless, forced options do not of themselves generate drama. What distinguishes Job (and wins him divine accolades in the end) also reveals the corrective operative in the book itself. By addressing himself to the author of the covenant, rather than debating its terms with those purportedly expert in it, Job grasps what his (ostensibly Israelite) friends have missed. The covenant itself is a gift bestowed personally by God on this people, thereby establishing a path by which they could come to realize that they are God's own people. By eluding the legal trap, Job subverts the legal context into which his friends have led him by recognizing a more encompassing context which the others fail to note. The ostensible judge is in fact the very One who originally gifted Israel with the covenant, so will only be shown proper gratitude by a direct address.

In the measure that the covenant is gift, it must be intended to lead those to whom it is given to the giver, rather than serve to veil the donor. Of all the protagonists, it is the one who is afflicted (not himself an Israelite) who displays his dignity and exercises his freedom by addressing the very One whom he acknowledges to be the agent of his affliction! In doing so, Job also bests the story's trickster figure, who so astutely articulated the weakness endemic to the theology which that framing story presumes (and which Job's friends repeat ad nauseam). Satan proposes, in effect, "If you (God) always reward those who obey you, you will never be able to know why they are doing it."

Through his audacity, Job is freed from the tyranny of a conceptual and existential bind—existential because it is so conceptually abstract. Absent the culminating response of his divine interlocutor, however, he could not have been freed, but would be left alone with audacity (as his interlocutors never cease to insist). So the freedom which he comes to enjoy is hardly an achievement, but can be enjoyed only as a gift. And the joy is that much sweeter for having been forged out of an intolerable suffering. It is so sweet, indeed, that he need not rejoice in his interlocutors' defeat so much as in having discovered—for himself and (thanks to the poet) for others—a way out of the bind their conceptual constraints could only reinforce.

What could have fueled such audacity? Nothing, I would suggest, but the promise that his pleas would find a hearing and elicit a reply to which he could respond. Job's outspokenness, which his staunchly orthodox interlocutors took to be an insistent claim, was rather a plea to be recognized by the very One whose recognition could liberate him from their unyielding logic and from his own terrible physical torment. That liberating gift came in the divine response—less in the words the poet had to construct for the One to speak than in the very fact that such a One responded at all.

What more could one dare ask? Had an explanation been given, could he or we have comprehended it? That question is indeed answered in the tenor of the poet's constructed response, which could be read as a cosmic rebuff to Job himself, but in the light of the closing commendation has to be seen as a reminder—to all who would explain the ways of God to human beings—that "as the heavens are higher than the earth, so are my ways higher than your ways and my thoughts than your thoughts" (Isaiah 55:9).

Now we can begin to imagine the freedom one experiences on being liberated from having to undertake such futile explanations, and freed precisely by the approval of the "lord of heaven and earth." As we might have suspected, if the book of Job serves the philosophical purpose of deconstructing pretentious claims to theodicy, it will turn out to be a philosophical work, much as Kierkegaard's celebrated subversion of the potted Hegelian "system" astutely employs philosophical strategies to effect his ostensibly "anti-philosophical" intent. By exposing how straightforward transactional discourse inevitably misconstrues the ineffable relationship of creatures to their creator, the book of Job leads us indirectly yet ineluctably into that analogous mode of discourse which alone can elucidate the distinction of creator from creatures.[8]

It is precisely that mode of discourse that has been intimated throughout this inquiry, by showing how authentically free action always portends *more* than the commonplace idiom of *choosing* can convey. Moreover, it has proved natural to display that difference by overtly theological references, as if to corroborate John Milbank's observation that "authentic metaphysics must be theological."[9] We have been moved in that direction, as we expounded the classical picture of freedom as *responding*, in the face of the unexplained *initiating* presumed by modernist libertarian theories of freedom. This naturally led from "Responding to what?" ("The Good") for Plato, to "Responding to Whom?"

for Abrahamic traditions. This is hardly an ineluctable path, of course, but it is a plausible one, provided one can embrace the asseveration of free creation which those traditions elaborate.

Imaginations formed by the New Testament are drawn spontaneously from Job to Jesus—notably, from Job's torment and liberation to Jesus' passion and resurrection. Now the gospel narratives presume an intimate relationship between Jesus and "the Father," operative in plaintive cries: "Abba, Father, all things are possible to you; remove this cup from me, yet not what I will, but what you will" (Mark 14:16) and at the moment of his death, "My God, my God, why have you forsaken me?" (15:34). Unlike Job's ceaseless searching, however, that relationship, while effective throughout Jesus' life, remains utterly inaccessible to us. Yet we can find it mirrored in Jesus' interaction which his disciples, and theirs with him, as that relationship is poignantly illustrated in the passion and resurrection narratives.

Staying with Mark's account, whose unadorned prose has a way of displaying the unvarnished truth, we find his disciples' obtuseness epitomized in Peter's presumptive reaction to Jesus' imminent prediction, "You will all fall away." Peter asserts, "Even though they all fall away, I will not." Jesus responds to this by again predicting, "This very night, before the cock crows twice, you will deny me three times," and Peter retorts "vehemently, 'if I must die with you, I will not deny you.' And they all said the same" (Mark 14: 27–31). What Jesus predicted did of course come to pass. Peter did deny him, after which, "he broke down and wept" (Mark 14:72), and none of his chosen apostles appear among the "many . . . women who came up with him to Jerusalem [and were] looking on from afar" (15:40–41) at the scene of his crucifixion. In short, they all had "fallen away" by escaping that fateful moment.

Yet even when we know this disheartening outcome, we are hardly prepared for the way Mark depicts the risen Jesus' consternation at their reaction to the news of his resurrection, as he imbeds it in the finale to his gospel: "He appeared to the eleven themselves as they sat at table; and he upbraided them for their unbelief and hardness of heart, because they had not believed those who saw him after he had risen" (Mark 16:14). It is true that Jesus immediately charges them: "Go into all the world and preach the gospel to the whole creation," but to understand what that portends, we need to recapitulate this dramatic denouement.

Everyone knows how discerning, even cagey, are the resurrection narratives. And all of them—yet, especially Mark—privilege the women disciples over the chosen apostles:

> And when the Sabbath was past, Mary Magdalene and Mary the mother of James, and Salome, brought spices, so that they might go and anoint him. And very early on the first day of the week, they went to the tomb when the sun had risen. And they were saying to one another, "Who will roll away the stone for us from the door of the tomb?" And looking up, they saw that the stone was rolled back—it was very large. And entering the tomb they saw a young man sitting on the right side, dressed in a white robe; and they were amazed. And he said to them: "Do not be amazed; you seek Jesus of Nazareth, who was crucified. He has risen, he is not here; see the place where they laid him. But go, tell his disciples and Peter that he is going before you to Galilee; there you will see him, as he told you." And they went out and fled from the tomb, for trembling and astonishment had come upon them; and they said nothing to anyone, for they were afraid (Mark 16:1–8).

At this very point, New Revised Standard Version notes, "some of the most ancient authorities bring the book to a close." So the apostles would not even have figured in those versions—to be upbraided or commissioned! In that case, Mark's privileging of the women as witnesses would be even more notable. Staying with the extended version—

as subsequently accepted by the Church—we can ask ourselves what this "good news" they were commissioned to
"peach to the whole creation" would be like. And we could
hardly escape answering that it would have to include their
"unbelief and hardness of heart," with which Mark con-
cludes his narrative.

So Jesus' humiliation on the cross was not merely to be
related, but was to be intensified in *their* humiliation as they
sought to escape its implications for themselves; his glorious resurrection would be mirrored in their inglorious un-
willingness to accept what the women had witnessed. Upbraided by the very one whom they had failed to follow to
the end, they were now enjoined to preach a message inviting others to follow him when they had failed to do so themselves.

What could make this "good news" good? It was the fact,
of course, that they were nonetheless enjoined to preach it—
and "not as servants but as friends" (John 15:15). The very
ones who had failed to accept the women's witness were
themselves sent to give witness to a death they had avoided
and a resurrection which they could not accept, which they
could only preach "with broken and contrite hearts" (Psalm
51). There is no triumph here. But is not that what makes the
news good—for them and for all who would hear the message so transmitted over multiple generations?

Freed from having to be heroes, their preaching could
liberate others from having to achieve what they themselves
had had to initiate. The very form of the preaching could
help those who heard it to be receptive of the gift, and to
find in that gift the freedom to respond. Again, without Job
or Jesus, we would be constrained to think of our freedom
as initiating, but with them we can discover freedom in responding.

CHAPTER FOUR

Philosophical Presumptions
and Strategies Clarified by Theology

Whoever can countenance the fact of free actions will spontaneously take them to be paradigms for agency. Yet the very notion of agency is itself contested. And to the extent that it evokes origination, we can begin to see why early Mu'tazalites would presume free agents to mimic the pattern of free creation. They both seem to be unencumbered by antecedent conditions, for however many antecedents the free actions of creatures may acknowledge, these cannot even jointly determine the action we deem to be free. By contrast, however, a free creator must be totally free of any conditions extrinsic to divine wisdom itself.

Nevertheless, it may prove to be true that one cannot secure human freedom without acknowledging a radically free creation. George Steiner took a similar tack when he argued that the author of nature will be needed to authenticate any human author.[1] His foil was, of course, the structuralist penchant to totally expunge authorial status, which Steiner endorsed in the absence of a free creator. Inverting an argument made by Dorothy Sayers—in *The Mind of the Maker*[2]—who uses the author/character analogy to illuminate that of creator/creature, Steiner insists on a divine author to validate human authorial claims. I am attempting to do the same for claims of human freedom.

The argument is three-fold. First, it counters the presumption of autonomy, which postulates an unexplained initiative to contrast free actions with actions otherwise caused—the libertarian presumption. Second, it argues that construing human freedom as a response to a good independent of it, rather than as an initiative ex nihilo, offers a more plausible delineation of free actions as we know them. Third, it offers an account of that good as origin as

31

well as goal; its free origination validates what freedom creatures can claim for themselves.

We have seen the first two points articulated in our inquiry thus far. Now let us focus on the third. The origin and validation of human freedom has its origin in a free creator. There is no freedom without creation; there are no free agents without a free creator. Consequently, we are constrained to elucidate free creation, as best we can, in an effort to offer a coherent account of human freedom.[3]

Let us turn to an axial figure in Christian philosophical theology, yet one who himself turned to Jewish and Islamic thinkers to help express the dynamic latent in the unique relation of creature to creator.[4] Aquinas's capacity to integrate philosophical with theological demands is displayed in the article, the *Summa Theologiae*'s treatment of creation: "Must everything that is have been caused by God?"[5] Relying on his earlier identification of God as that One whose very essence is to exist,[6] Aquinas shows why one must "necessarily say that whatever in any way *is* is from God." If "God is sheer existence subsisting of its very nature (*ipsum esse per se subsistens*), [and so] must be unique . . . then it follows that all things other than God are not their own existence but share in existence."[7] So the Neo-Platonic distinction between essential and participated being is invoked to give everything but the creator the stamp of created. Very little, if anything, is said here about causation, but the elements are in place to press for a unique form of it, even though another way of posing the initial question employs Aristotle explicitly: Is God the efficient cause of all beings?

An objection asks about those "natural necessities" which Aristotle presumed simply to be, or always to have been: "Since there are many such in reality [such as spiritual substances and heavenly bodies which carry no principle of dissolution within themselves], all beings are not from God." Aquinas deftly diverts this objection by recalling the primacy of existing: "An active cause is required not simply because the effect could not be [that is, it is contingent], but because the effect would not be if the cause were not [existing]."[8]

Even necessary things will require a cause for their very being; this is a radical revision of Aristotle, depending on the Avicennian distinction of essence from existing. What it suggests is that Aquinas was seeking for a way of understanding created being using Aristotelian metaphysics, yet the "givens" of that philosophy would have to be transformed to meet the exigency of a free creator. Put another way, which anticipates our elucidation, the being which Aristotle took to characterize substance had to become (for Aquinas) an *esse ad creatorem* (an existing in relation to the creator). This is another way of saying that all things other than God are not their own existence, neither in the radical sense on which this article insists, distinguishing creatures from the creator, nor in the more attenuated sense in which the being which they have cannot be "their own"—belonging to them "by right" or by virtue of their being the kind of things they are (which is Aristotle's view).

Everything other than God receives its being from the creator as a gift. Yet such derived or participated things are no less real than Aristotle's substances, since now there is no other way to be except to participate in the *ipsum esse* of the creator. As a consequence, the nature of the creating act depends crucially on our conception of the One from whom *all that is* comes.

Now if that One is most properly identified as "He who is" since "the existence of God is his essence and since this is true of nothing else," then we are in the presence of One whose characteristic act will be "to produce existence [*esse*] absolutely . . . which belongs to the meaning of creation" defined as "the emanation of the whole of being from a universal cause" or "universal being."[9] That being's "proper effect," then, is the very existence of things.[10] One implication of this unique form of causation is that "creation is not a change, except merely according to our way of understanding, [since] creation, whereby the entire substance of things is produced, does not allow of some common subject now different from what it was before, except according to our way of understanding which conceives an object as first not existing at all and afterwards as existing."[11]

Creating is not a process answering the question: *How* does God create? God creates intentionally, that is, by intellect and will, though these are identical in God. Thus, Aquinas has no difficulty adopting the metaphor of emanation to convey something of the act of creation—God's consenting to the universe coming forth from God, that One whose essence is simply to be.[12] The revelation of God's inner life as Father, Son, and Spirit will in fact allow Aquinas to say more, while respecting the absence of process.

It is this revelation which directs us to "the right idea of creation. The fact of saying that God made all things by His Word excludes the error of those who say that God produced things by necessity. When we say that in Him there is a procession of love, we show that God produced creatures not because He needed them, nor because of any other extrinsic reason, but on account of the love of His own goodness."[13] The act of creating, therefore, is not a "mere overflow" (or emanation) from this One whose very nature is to be. It is rather an intentional emanating and so a gracious gift. Yet the mode of action remains utterly consonant with the divine nature, hence the natural metaphor of emanation.

The other metaphor which Aquinas invokes is that of the artisan: "God's knowledge is the cause of things; for God's knowledge stands to all created things as the artist's to his products," with the implication that "natural things are suspended between God's [practical] knowledge and our [speculative] knowledge."[14] The deft way Aquinas employs Aristotle's distinction here, between practical and speculative knowing, allows him to utilize the metaphor of artisan critically, and so avoid pitting divine and human knowing against one another.

Since God's knowing brings things into being and sustains them, we need not worry about whether God's knowing what will happen determines future contingent events, since the knowing which God has of what will take place is not propositional in character. God knows what God does; the model is practical knowing. Taking a cue from Aquinas's strategy regarding God's knowledge of singulars, we must say that divine knowledge extends as far as divine activity, for God does not work mindlessly. Yet we can have no more determinate model for divine knowing than that.[15]

Nevertheless, the artisan metaphor for creation might lead one to suspect that the product could subsist without any further action on the part of its maker. Hence, emanation must be invoked to remind us of the revolution which the presence of a creator and the act of creation has worked in Aristotle: the very being (*esse*) of creatures is now an *esse-ad*, "a relation to the creator as the origin of its existence."[16] Aristotle's definition of substance as "what subsists in itself" can still function to distinguish substance from accident, but the being inherent to created substances proceeds from another, from the source who alone subsists eternally as the One whose essence is to be.

If substances must now be denominated "created substances," the causality associated with creating can hardly be comprehended among Aristotle's four causes. The two contenders—efficient and formal—each fail since an efficient cause without something to work on would be unintelligible to Aristotle. Moreover, trying to fit the creator into Aristotle's formal cause would directly foster pantheism, as Aquinas notes.[17] A "cause of being" must be sui generis, as we shall see, confirming the distinction of creator from creation, while the founding "non-reciprocal relation of dependence" must be unique as well, and best characterized by the borrowed expression "nonduality."[18] The practical knowing involved in creating is more like doing than making, suggesting James Ross's prescient image of the "being of the cosmos like a song on the breath of a singer," while emphasizing that "God's causing being can be analogous to many diverse things without even possibly being the same as any one of them."[19]

What a Free Creation Portends

We begin to see the philosophical thickets into which this assertion—that God freely creates the universe—can lead us. And rightly so, since that affirmation grounds all the other Abrahamic faiths as well. Indeed, both al-Ghazali and Moses Maimonides staunchly resisted the necessity endemic to the picture of creation as emanation—which they encountered in the philosophy of their time—for fear that it would preclude the very possibility of revelation. Nothing short of a free creation can ground a free revelation, and with it, a free human response to the One from whom all that is comes forth.[20]

Aquinas enlists the resources of Neo-Platonism to offer a philosophically coherent account of the creator as the One causing being, allowing him to insist that "the proper effect of the first and most universal cause, which is God, is existence itself (*ipsum esse*)."[21] But since this effect is that of an agent thoroughly intentional and free, he also insists that "what God principally intends in created things is that form which consists in the good of order of the universe" (*bonum ordinis universi*)."[22] Calling the "good of order of the universe" a form is clearly as much of an accommodation of Aristotelian terminology as calling the creator "the efficient cause of all being," yet the stretch must begin somewhere.[23] As always, one notices the transformation in the ways Aquinas employs these notions once they have been introduced; it is language in use which counts.

Since mention of good invites a discussion of evil, Aquinas's concluding remarks to this section on "the distinction among creatures"—including "the distinction between good and evil"—are especially illuminating. He is confronted with the Manichean argument that "we should postulate some supreme evil which of itself is the cause of evils [since were one to] allege that evil has an indirect cause merely, not a direct cause . . . it would follow that evil would crop up rarely, not frequently, as it in fact does."[24] His response is forthright:

As for the reference to evil being present in the majority of cases (*in pluribus*), it is simply untrue. For things subject to generation and decay, in which alone we experience physical evil, compose but a small part of the whole universe, and besides defects of nature are minority occurrences in any species. They seem to be in a majority only among human beings. For what appears good for them as creatures of sense is not simply good for them as human, that is as reasonable beings; in fact, most of them follow after sense, rather than intelligence.[25]

This sharp exchange can be parsed as Aquinas's countering the claim that there is more evil than good in the universe by means of a distinction: in the natural world—despite cataclysms, miscarriages, and other defects of nature—there is manifestly more good than evil in creation. Here his faith perspective is reinforced by his Aristotelian cosmology, as it would be even more by the intricacies unveiled by modern science. The human world, however, reflects the opposite state of affairs, to which Aquinas assigns a cause here, only to explore it later.[26] What might well startle us, however, is the matter-of-fact assertion that our cultural world displays more evil than good.

Aquinas would have had no truck with modernity's claim about human perfectibility, so he hardly needed the chastening of the twentieth century to disabuse him. He did feel the need to account for our role in systematically distorting creation, however, though our experience with the way that claims of human perfectibility have distorted the natural environment of humans could expand exponentially on his. Ironically, that hubris peculiar to humans can at least in part be traced to the way we find his earlier claim—that "things subject to generation and decay . . . compose but a small part of the whole universe"—so quaint. A universe bereft of higher intelligences, whether they be identified as heavenly bodies or angels, can only place human beings at its pinnacle, thus leading us to read that fatal line in Genesis as licensing us to transform the natural world to serve our needs.

Aquinas's lapidary explanation for this propensity of ours—that most of us "follow after sense rather than intelligence"— recalls the "good of order of the universe" as well, as he notes that this propensity also contravenes our given nature, since "what appears good for them as creatures of sense is not simply good for them as humans." Moreover, this is a humanity firmly placed within the "good of order of the universe" and hence included within a vast world of nature, indeed inserted at the point where the material and the spiritual dimensions of that universe intersect. This is an awesome picture indeed, and one Aquinas could glean from his Aristotelian cosmology, but can only be available to us by faith.

A Platonic Corollary: Participation

It is but a short step from this treatment to the central theme of participation in Aquinas's account of created being. Indeed, recognizing how central participation is to Aquinas's metaphysics of created being recalls Josef Pieper's penetrating observation that creation is "the hidden element in the philosophy of St. Thomas."[27] And registering the implications of Pieper's remark should lead one to re-assess the easy demarcation between philosophy and theology so redolent of twentieth-century Thomism.[28]

In a monograph of stunning proportions, Rudi te Velde offers a fresh presentation of this theme, recapitulating the earlier work of Cornelio Fabro (1950) and Louis Geiger (1952).[29] He begins his consideration of Aquinas's use of this Platonic notion with the apparently innocent question posed by Boethius in *De hebdomadibus* (on which Aquinas commented): How can things be said to be good—by participation or by substance? It is this disjunction that will bother Aquinas, and his commentary will make clear that Boethius must pose it that way because for him "participation refers to an accidental property of a substance," depending as it does "on the Aristotelian categorical division of being into substance and accident."[30] Boethius's solution—that things are good "in virtue of [their] relation to the first Good"—leaves us asking "in what sense created things are good by participation, such that they are nevertheless also essentially and not just accidentally good."[31]

So the issue is joined: participation will need to be explicated by an ontology richer than the received distinction of substance/accident, although the mode of participation operative in that very distinction will offer us some hints as to how to understand it in a fuller way. The next step, articulated in *De veritate* 21, will carry us from good to being. And it will be crucial to establish that these two transcendentals are convertible, since at first blush they look so different. (Something may be said to *be* simply by virtue of its being present, while we only call a fully developed thing good.) What will unite them is Aquinas's insistence that "everything is perfect insofar as it is actual (*in actu*)," so that by "identifying act as the proper *ratio* of being" he can assert, "That by which a thing is understood as a being—its actuality—is the same as what makes it a desirable object."[32]

We can begin to see how Aquinas transforms participation as he found it, offering an interpretation of the Neo-Platonic hierarchy which will not include God as part of it, while incorporating the Aristotelian notion of form in such a way as "to reconcile his metaphysical gradualism, based on participation, with the substantiality of created beings."[33] Both Hellenic streams will be transformed to show that there is "but one transcendent source of participation from which all things derive their distinct perfection."[34] Moreover, the unity of those perfections in God, to offer a rich evocation of divine unity as metaphysical simpleness, completes the account by returning to the plenitude of Aquinas's understanding of *esse*.

What work does this rich new notion of participation accomplish, and how does it uniquely reflect Aquinas's methodological strategy? Rudi te Velde's concluding remarks put this clearly:

> Thomas does not place himself on a standpoint prior to creation in order to reconstruct from God's point of view how the actual creation has taken place, first by conceiving the finite essences of things and then by granting them actual existence outside God. Rather his approach is to inquire into the intelligible ground of things starting from the world as it is. He questions the whole of reality in the light of being. In order to account for their being, all things should be reduced to what is primary in the order of being, to God as *prima causa*. From the being of things this cause must be understood as *ipsum esse*, the origin of all the perfection found in reality. . . . Although it is one single act whereby God necessarily wills his own goodness *and* other things because of his goodness, in relation to these other things, God's will is free creative love.[35]

Creator and Creatures—a Nonduality?

A more theological commentary on these matters can be found in the slim volume of Teape lectures by Sara Grant, recently re-issued by Bradley Malkovsky: *Towards an Alternative Theology: Confessions of a Non-dualist Christian*.[36] She says,

> In India as in Greece, the ultimate question must always be that of the relation between the supreme unchanging Reality and the world of coming-to-be and passing away, the eternal Self and what appears as non-Self, and no epistemology can stand secure as long as this question remains unanswered. . . . A systematic study of Ankara's use of relational terms made it quite clear to me that he agrees with St. Thomas Aquinas in regarding the relation between creation and the ultimate Source of all being as a non-reciprocal depen-

dence relation; i.e., a relation in which subsistent effect or "relative absolute" is dependent on its cause for its very existence as a subsistent entity, whereas the cause is in no way dependent on the effect for its subsistence, though there is a necessary logical relation between cause and effect; i.e., a relation which is perceived by the mind when it reflects on the implications of the existence of the cosmos.

Her final observation about a "necessary logical relation" is quite compatible with regarding creating as a free action of the creator, for its import is intended to capture Aquinas's identification of "creation in the creature [as] nothing other than a relation of sorts to the creator as the principle of its existing."[37]

So the very existence (*esse*) of a creature is an *esse-ad*, an existing which is itself a relation to its source. As we have noted, nothing could better express the way in which Aquinas's formulation of the essence/existing distinction transforms Aristotle than to point out that what for Aristotle "exists in itself" (substance) is for Aquinas derived from an Other in its very in-itselfness, or substantiality. Since the Other is the cause of being, each thing which "exists to" the creator also exists in itself. Derived existence is no less substantial when it is derived from the One who is, so it would appear that one could succeed in talking of existing things without explicitly referring them to their source. "The distinction," in other words, need not appear. But that simply reminds us how unique a nonreciprocal relation of dependence must be; it characterizes one relation only, that of creatures to creator.

If creator and creature were distinct from each other in an ordinary way, the relation—even one of dependence—could not be nonreciprocal; ordinarily, the fact that something receives its being from an originating agent, as a child from a parent, must mark a difference in that agent itself. Yet the fact that a cause of being, properly speaking, is not affected by causing all that is does not imply remoteness or uncaring—indeed, quite the opposite. Such a One must cause in such a way as to be present in each creature as that to which it is oriented in its very existing. In that sense, this One cannot be considered as *other* than what it creates, in an ordinary sense of that term—just as the creature's *esse-ad* assures that it cannot *be* separately from its source.[38] So it will not work simply to contrast creation to emanation, or to picture the creator distinct (in the ordinary sense) from creation by contrast with a more pantheistic image. Indeed, it is to avoid such infelicities of imagination that Sara Grant has recourse to Sankara's sophisticated notion of nonduality—to call our attention in an arresting way to the utter uniqueness of "the distinction" which must indeed hold between creator and creation, but cannot be pictured in any contrastive manner.[39]

Nor does Aquinas feel any compunction at defining creation as the "emanation of all of being from its universal cause (*emanatio totius entis a cause universali*)."[40] Indeed, once he had emptied the emanation scheme of any mediating role, he could find no better way of marking the uniqueness of the causal relation of creation than by using the term *emanation* to articulate it.[41] Once the scheme has been gutted, that "sui generis" descriptor should serve to divert us from imagining the creator "over against" the universe, as an entity exercising causal efficacy on anything that is in a manner parallel to causation within the universe.[42] While this all-important distinction preserves God's freedom in creating, which the emanation scheme invariably finesses, we must nevertheless be wary of picturing that distinction in a fashion which assimilates the creator to another item within the universe. Harm Goris has shown how close attention to the uniqueness of the creator/creature relation, with its attendant corollary of participation as a way of articulating this sui generis causal relation, can neutralize many of the conundrums which fascinate philosophers of religion.[43]

Although it may seem that we have strayed far from Aquinas in invoking Shakara's hybrid term, *nonduality*, we should have realized by now how Aquinas helps himself to various ways of expressing the inexpressible—for example, the distinction as well as the relation between creatures and their creator. Both prove to be foundational to any attempt to grasp our transcendent origins as gift. Bible and Qur'an conspire to highlight the creator's freedom; philosophy proves helpful in thinking about both creature and creator together, in a way that is empowering rather than threatening.

CHAPTER FIVE

How Narrative Contextualizes
and Articulates Freedom:
Augustine and Etty Hillesum

IN ATTEMPTING TO ASSESS the authenticity of our thoughtful
decisions, we ought not to approach them as though they
offer explanations, but rather name them for what they are:
convictions—convictions that there is a sense to it all, not
that *we* can make sense of it all. What fuels such convictions
is one's growing capacity to use a language which helps us
progressively gain our bearings in the midst of a journey.
(The image of journey comes quite naturally to Jews, Christians, or Muslims—where the Exodus, Jesus' "setting his
face towards Jerusalem" (Luke 9:51), or the Hegira and the
hajj offer ready paradigms for the faithful.) Unlike an explanatory framework, this language is one into which we
are called to enter if we would allow our life to become a
journey. And the promise of undertaking such a journey is
not only sense or direction for our lives, but sense for it all.

So the communal and cosmic dimensions are para-
mount, though accentuating the first can threaten the scope
of the promise by restricting it to a faith community, while
cosmic assertions tempt us to misconstrue faith assertions
as explanations. We can be helped to avoid both misreadings by focusing on anyone called upon to make sense
of their life, and the manner in which it must be done—
namely, by telling their story. Our guides will be two—one
classical and the other contemporary, a man and a woman, a Christian and a Jew—Aurelius Augustine and Etty
Hillesum. The first is a powerful figure of history, a prolific
author and ecclesiastical leader, loved and maligned for the

considerable influence his long life and manifold writings have exerted over the centuries. The second is known only to those whom her published diaries and letters have admitted into her truncated life, yet one, a victim of genocide, who forged a vision that carries us well beyond victimhood. It is in fact their similarities, as seekers and finders, which this essay shall explore—the differences in their faith communities only enhancing that project.[1]

Augustine opens his *Confessions* asserting, "We are among your creatures, Lord, and our instinct is to praise you. . . . The thought of you stirs us so deeply that we cannot be content unless we praise you, because you made us for yourself and our hearts find no peace until they rest in you."[2] These words begin a reflective introduction of five short chapters to a work which offered the West a paradigm for autobiography. Yet it differs from more modern autobiographies in its form of address and its attribution of agency. It frequently shifts from first to second person, as its author is moved to praise, since the narrative activity of remembering is less preoccupied with what happened to Augustine, and how Augustine negotiated it, than with (1) identifying the sources of power and, once located, (2) learning how to receive from that source. If *autobiography*, like *autonomy*, suggests to us a self centered on itself, Augustine's journey delivers a self related to its source and so ordered in itself—since to be related to one's source and goal *is* to be properly ordered with oneself. Seeking and receiving are reciprocally related, since recognizing what and who that source is orients one to the proper ways to receive from it.

If the self Augustine articulates is not autonomous but related, the form of his articulation is dialogic. How are the two—form and substance—related? My interpretive hypothesis asks us to attend to three factors—each of them features of the work. The first is a simple reminder that introductions are written once we have finished composing, for only then can we confidently say where we wish to go. Therefore, the assertion which introduces the narrative— a second-person assertion at that—is best thought of as the

fruit of the efforts required to articulate his journey of relating. Here is my second premise: those efforts comprise
an experiment—that is, an account of a life becomes an experiment in truth, while the narrative mode of accounting
enhances the experiment by articulating it for us. Finally,
the response of God to Augustine's sustained yet fitful outreach is exhibited in the life itself—that is, in what God accomplished in him by way of right ordering. Book 10 offers
a current "progress report" on that transformation, replete
with Augustine's disappointment at its incompleteness. Yet
the fact of what has been accomplished encourages him to
move beyond his own narrative to the cosmic commentary
of Books 11–13, thereby offering the ground for his opening
assertion: "Man is one of your creatures, Lord, and his instinct is to praise you."

So the propriety of the dialogic form of the narrative-
recollection which is the *Confessions* is corroborated as the
reality of each partner comes more into evidence through
exercises in dialogue—Augustine speaking, God working.
What is more, each one is seen to be dialogic in nature.
With God, the dialogue is reflected more in God's interaction with creation than within divinity itself (as in his *de
Trinitate*); with Augustine, it is exhibited primarily in communal exchange with friends, with Monica, and with his
son.[3] This feature of his narrative, notably evident after he
leaves Africa for Italy, reminds us forcibly that this "autobiography" does not render an autonomous individual but a
person in community.[4]

The character of that community proves to be the crucial middle term in the verification which Augustine seeks
in trying to identify accurately the source of right order, ca-
pable of restoring himself and the world to its original ordering. He comes to see how participating in such a community offers the most promising hope for attaining an
ordered self, as its teachings offer a paradigm for assessing
alternative accounts of world order—hence the apt observation of readers who have seen in this work the itinerary of a
journey towards "joining the Church." To demonstrate what

kind of a community it is which he embraces (and by which he *is* embraced), he does not direct us to historical "proofs." He directs us to ask this question: What sort of life does the community exhibit? The response, especially of Book 8, is that it generates saints, exemplary individuals who display an enviable ordering in their lives.[5] The community can be said to generate them, since we find this ordering in people who identify themselves as followers of Jesus. It is an ordering, moreover, which exemplifies the best of human nature, yet is all too seldom exemplified in individual human beings. They testify to the presence and activity of the original orderer of the world, as well as to the further fact that individuals can relate to such a One: "You made us for yourself and our hearts find no peace until they rest in you."

So much for the structure of the *Confessions*. How does it work? That, of course, is what the narrative is designed to show, in *his* case. But what about us? What if our story—yours or mine—does not so conclude? Is that not the way with stories, in principle? They are not, we know, universal.

Or are there certain ones which are paradigmatic for the rest of us? Archetypal even, so that we cannot escape incorporation into their plot? These would be "everyman" stories, enlightening us regarding our origins and our destiny. But even if we would admit such stories, would Augustine's *Confessions* be among them? Can his story be archetypal, however much some of us would like it to be?

Here it is useful to contrast the direction Augustine's journey took with a path it could have taken, at the penultimate milestone of the journey towards discovery. His is not an account, as the story of his Platonist guides would be, of the necessary ascent of a human soul to its inherent perfection, impeded only by willful inattention or blindness.[6] It rather spells out a free response to an invitation freely offered to each person and avowedly to all, yet the story unfolds into a willing response seen as contained within a dynamic initiated by the Other.

The narrative-recollection, as Augustine offers it, may be paradigmatic but is not archetypal. That is, it can help to structure your story, but it cannot be said to structure it inescapably. So it is not only experimental in Augustine's case; it is inherently experimental. Try it on, to see whether your story can be modeled upon it. The *promise* is that yours will be able so to be modeled, if you try.

The incentive lies in your observation that those who have, and are otherwise like you, exhibit an enviable ordering, so why not try? At least, those who participate in the same community as Augustine did hope that incentive is present. If that is all we can glean from this exercise with Augustine, however, we ask, "To what end?" There seems to be little, if anything, new here. What has our study of the form and function of Augustine's *Confessions* succeeded in showing?

In answer, I shall suggest two things which may be more therapeutic than startling. The first regards the indispensability of narrative, especially first-person narrative, in framing an account of an invitation offered freely so that it elicits a willing response. Any other form of discourse, it seems, will tend to eclipse the free dynamic of invitation and response in favor of a mode of explanation. The second is a corollary of the first. It posits the centrality of friendship and of dialogue in human life, opening one up to the possibility—indeed, the fact—of such an exchange with the one source of all.

The shorthand expression for such a relationship with God is "grace," and the contrast which Augustine finds between his Platonist guides and those who witness faith in Jesus as the word of God (epitomized in the tonal differences between Books 7 and 8 of the *Confessions*) displays the novelty which he discovers grace to be. Moreover, the fruit of that new power in his personal life is a transformed vision of the world itself, where all things have "the same message to tell, if only we can hear it, and their message is this: We did not make ourselves, but [the One] who abides forever made us."[7] Having negotiated the journey he recounts, Augustine is now able to hear this response from the things whose beauty he admires.[8]

A similar refrain, rooted more explicitly in her own feelings, yet no less cosmic in scope and import, punctuates the diaries and letters of Etty Hillesum.[9] Less structured than Augustine's self-conscious "confessions," Hillesum's spontaneously reflective entries document a person seeking to center and order her life, who one day finds herself "forced to the ground by something stronger than myself. . . . I suddenly went down on my knees in the middle of this large room . . . almost automatically."[10] The consequences of that action, in the context of her interaction with Julius Spier, her psychoanalyst and intimate friend, lead her inner life to unfold to the point where she can say (even in the midst of the misery of Westerbork, a staging area for transport to Auschwitz), "time and again it soars straight from my heart—I can't help it, that's just the way it is, like some elementary force—the feeling that life is glorious and magnificent."[11]

That feeling is not ephemeral, but a power making her over from within: "[As] the threat grows ever greater, and terror increases from day to day, I draw prayer round me like a dark protective wall . . . and then step outside again, calmer and stronger."[12] "It always spreads from the inside outwards with me."[13] This courage is displayed by one who confesses, "I have never been able to 'do' anything; I can only let things take their course and, if need be, suffer"[14]— an apt remark from a woman who sought therapy shortly after her twenty-seventh birthday, sensing a void in herself and her relationships.

"I am . . . just about seasoned enough, I should think, to be counted among the better lovers, and love does indeed suit me to perfection, and yet . . . deep inside me something is still locked away."[15] So runs the opening paragraph of her diaries—plausibly a task given her, as a catalyst to their inner work, by the man whom she had sought out, Julius Spier. What follows in her writing can usefully be divided into three roughly even parts: her discovery of herself through the relationship with Spier,[16] a period of preparation for serving others,[17] and the actual crafting of her life as gift.[18] The final phase begins at this point, where all illusions are torn away: "What is at stake is our impending destruction and annihilation,"[19] and is focused by the death of the guide whom she had come to love: "You taught me to speak the name of God without embarrassment. You were the mediator . . . and now . . . my path leads straight to God. . . . And I shall be the mediator for any other soul I can reach."[20]

These remarks were written after she had volunteered to accompany the first group of Jews being sent to Westerbork. They are rooted in the second, preparatory phase, however, when she discovers, encountering a former lover, that "everything is no longer pure chance . . . an exciting adventure. Instead I have the feeling that I have a destiny, in which the events are strung significantly together."[21] Less than two months later, she will assert, "I have matured enough to assume my 'destiny,' to cease living an accidental life."[22] What happens in her happens in a scant two-and-a-half years as the restrictive legislation bars "Jews from the paths and the open country [yet] I find life beautiful and I feel free. The sky within me is as wide as the one stretching above my head. I believe in God and I believe in man and I can say so without embarrassment."[23]

It is at the end of this period that she begins to formulate expressly theological dicta, in the face of "the latest news . . . that all Jews will be transported out of Holland . . . to Poland": "And yet I don't think life is meaningless. And God is not accountable to us for the senseless harm we cause one another. We are accountable to Him! I have already died a thousand deaths in a thousand concentration camps. . . . And yet I find life beautiful and meaningful. From minute to minute."[24] This capacity for gratitude and praise which she finds within herself moves her in this period of formation beyond humiliation or hate to a newfound peace and freedom: "Despite all the suffering and injustice, I cannot hate others."[25] "One day I shall surely be able to say to Ilse Blumenthal, 'Do not relieve your feelings through hatred, do not seek to be avenged on all German mothers. . . . Give your sorrow all the space and shelter in yourself that is its due . . . then you may truly say: 'Life is beautiful and so rich . . . that it makes you want to believe in God.'"[26]

Yet the God in whom Etty comes to believe is one to whom she introduces us in an entry which takes the form of a prayer: "Dear God, these are anxious times . . . but one thing is becoming increasingly clear to me: that you cannot help us, that we must help you to help ourselves . . . Alas, there doesn't seem to be much You Yourself can do about our circumstances, our lives. Neither do I hold you responsible. You cannot help us but we must help You and defend your dwelling place inside us to the last."[27] The responsibility she feels is to what has happened within her, and so to the world to which she has come to relate with all that she has. She writes from Westerbork, in the epilogue to the edition of her diaries, "I see more and more that love for all our neighbors . . . must take pride of place over love for one's nearest and dearest."[28] The reason is offered in a prayer from her diary which she shares with her friend Tide: "You have made me so rich, oh God, please let me share out Your beauty with open hands. My life has become an uninterrupted dialogue with You, oh God, one great dialogue."[29]

So the pattern of Augustine's *Confessions* is realized anew: the ability of each partner comes more into evidence through exercises in dialogue—Etty recording what God is accomplishing in her. In fact, what gives her account its authenticity is not only what she finds herself able to do—in the midst of indescribable misery[30]—but also that her capacities come as a continual surprise to herself. Just as Augustine's crafted narrative offered a confession of praise to the One who brought order out of his disorder, so Etty Hillesum's more spontaneous diaries celebrate the unlocking of "what is truly essential, and deep inside me,"[31] and the consequent transformation of a "miserable, frightened creature"[32] into a "soul . . . forged out of fire and rock crystal."[33] Hers is a soul, moreover, shaped by "an uninterrupted dialogue" which allowed her to make us the gift of her "interrupted life."

Some hermeneutical remarks would seem in order, for it is the life and deeds of someone like Etty which offer us a key to understanding what it is she says, as well as re-marking on the authenticity of the relationships which she recounts. Her transformation is palpable to us as well as to herself, through the largely transparent medium of per-sonal journals. Augustine, on the contrary, has acquired an immense persona over the course of fifteen centuries, and was already enough of a celebrity to need to craft his story with rhetorical skill. Yet *what* he confesses is what Etty cel-ebrates: a real alteration testifying to a real power at work in the world. Each of them is able to identify that power as the source of all that is, Augustine explicitly and Etty by her transformed vision: "It still all comes down to the same thing: life is beautiful. And I believe in God—right in the thick of what people call 'horror.'"[34] She addresses these words to her friend, by way of insisting that such a reality is accessible to that friend (Jopie) as well.

Indeed, what impresses one about Etty's diaries is the precise way in which they articulate a conviction shared by Jew and Christian alike—that life itself, indeed the uni-verse, is a gift. A friend, Klaas, whom she introduces as a "dogged old class fighter"—that is, a confirmed Marxist—was indeed "dismayed and astonished at the same time," and challenged her: "But that . . . that is nothing but Chris-tianity!" Her response is one we will by now have come to expect: "And I, amused by your confusion, retort quite cool-ly: 'Yes, Christianity, and why ever not?'"[35] For the histori-cally pockmarked relations between Judaism and Christian-ity, I believe this response touches a profound nerve, but for present purposes, let us simply take it that she has hit upon a shared conviction—that life is a gift.[36] That will suffice to allow us some fruitful reflections on the way in which such convictions function in transforming lives.

If one focuses on "the experience itself"—whatever that might be—of transformation, then the accounts may be contingently related to what it is that we cannot help but observe in the person before us. But when we are privileged enough to have access to the narrative account, we come to appreciate how it is that these narratives are shaped by sets of convictions which can otherwise be expressed as doctrines of specific religious traditions. Correlatively, the fact that doctrines shape narratives reminds us that they do not play a theoretical but a *grammatical* role in the lives of the faithful.[37] They do not, in short, offer explanatory access to a reality behind the One to whom individuals like Etty or Augustine respond, but rather provide the manner in which their respective responses offer us access to the reality revealed in their transformations.

Doctrine, in other words, both comes to life and is embodied in the response of those whom we cannot but recognize to be saints. It is obvious enough how doctrine comes to life there. But how can we say that it is embodied in such lives? The argument here is at once simple and subtle. It turns on the fact that we will always be forced to speak of religious matters in a language which is inherently analogous. The term *transformation* offers a handy example. Any formula we give for it will contain terms of a like quality— terms whose open texture or systematic ambiguity will demand that we offer an example to establish our frame of reference or benchmark usage.[38] And it is precisely individuals which provide the living examples to anchor our usage— a commonplace yet remarkable situation which accounts for the fact that we can recognize such exemplary individuals without always being able to *say* what it is that makes them such. Yet their narrative accounts, when available, can be found to be structured in such a way as to be shaped by what we otherwise call doctrinal statements. That is the way in which their lives embody doctrine.

What, then, are we to do with the further fact that distinct lives may embody diverse doctrines, and yet each exhibits a comparable transformation? (We may even presume that their respective accounts can be shown to embody different doctrinal positions.) Celebrate it, I contend, for (so far) we have no way of placing ourselves in the position of comparing or ranking religious traditions. I am not pontificating, insisting that we cannot do so; in fact, I suspect that we must. I am only remarking that we are not *yet* in a position to do so. We must acquire a set of intellectual skills allowing us to compare cultural frameworks. In fact, nothing, so effectively displays the cultural particularity of Christianity as the emergence of a post-colonial world, in which Western Christians found themselves facing other religious traditions but were no longer able to presume an accustomed superiority.

Karl Rahner, in a prescient lecture given at Boston College, and published in 1979, adduced cumulative evidence to propose 1970 as a threshold comparable to that marked by the destruction of the temple in Jerusalem in 70—the date usually associated with the parting of the ways between Jews and Christians.[39] Rahner shows how these two symbolic dates each mark a theological threshold, in which questions arise which outstrip the resources of the theologies of the day to handle. Indeed, Paul's struggles to make room for an emerging Hellenic community of believers without forfeiting his own heritage underscores Rahner's thesis.

Whenever subsequent writers sought to attenuate that struggle by offering a more plausible account, it turned out invariably that a "new" covenant replaced the "old," betraying both Jews and Christians, since Jews were thereby denied any theological lebensraum and Christians were deprived of their shaping heritage. So if we have been unable to offer a nondialectical account of that relationship, how should we expect to be ready to confront the current radical religious and cultural diversity? Yet Rahner's essay does offer both solace and direction: solace because we can appreciate ourselves to be standing in a liminal situation and realize that we will probably be posing the questions in an inadequate manner, and direction, in that his periodization reminds us that the western European phase of Christianity is over.

How are we to respond conceptually to such novelty? By reminding ourselves, I would suggest, that responses are structured by traditions whose doctrinal patterns provide the grammar of the response. Insofar as those doctrinal patterns shape and give direction to a lived response so that it issues in an authentic transformation, then we must acknowledge them to be true—just as the aim and correlative skills of an archer allow his arrow to find its mark. This strategy keeps us from directly comparing statements lifted out of different traditions, and reminds us that such statements—if they be religious statements—subserve that transforming relationship which we have noted in Etty and Augustine. Moreover, *within* each functioning tradition, there will be a set of such shaping beliefs or doctrines, the truth of which will (or will not) be exhibited in the life of the community, and especially in its notable exemplars. And where those exemplary individuals tell their story, as Augustine and Etty have, astute critics will be able to discern the doctrinal patterns which give their narratives a structure distinctive to the community in which they partake and the beliefs they hold. Such is the grammar of this matter: lives are rendered in narratives which display a structure. We are compelled by the lives, inspired and illuminated by the narratives, and guided by what we can discover of their structure.

What have we given up in trying to respond to the new situation of religious and cultural diversity? *Not* the "truth claims" of particular religious traditions, but rather a presumptive way of ranking them. *Not* the certainty which Newman attributes to faith, whereby we freely give "real assent" to what is offered us as liberating and life-giving, but a monocultural *attitude* of certainty in which we *know* we are right.[40] What we have recovered is an attitude of critical modesty towards our modes of expression—a critical modesty similarly displayed by medieval thinkers—which we can use to profit from a situation which appears so unsettling.

We have long overlooked just how intercultural and interreligious the medieval world really was.[41] I am referring to Aquinas's account of religious language, in which he used a sophisticated semantics to clarify and extend the views of Moses Maimonides on attributing perfections to divinity. The portion of that account pertinent here is Aquinas's insistence that phrases such as "God is just" can be said properly but imperfectly of divinity.[42]

By exploring how expressions might "imperfectly signify" divinity, we could be led to see how one tradition can be complemented by another, and so use the encounter with alternative conceptualities to enrich our own. That is, I believe, the sense of Etty's cool retort: "Yes, Christianity, and why ever not?" Far from a call to syncretism, that response appreciates the particular power of the gospels and appropriates them to her situation. These complementarities work quite well in practice, as the faithful in distinct traditions find themselves drawn to incorporate prayer patterns from one another, much as Jung remarked (in 1948) in reference to a division within western European Christianity, that every cultured European he knew was either a Catholic Protestant or a Protestant Catholic.[43]

But what of that further assessment, to which we seem inevitably drawn, which would compare traditions by ranking them? I have already noted that we are not yet in a position to do that. I say, "not yet"—not because I believe we may one day be able to, but to remind us how unskilled we are in comparing across cultural and conceptual frameworks. The immediate alternative of accepting the picture of religious traditions as several ways up one mountain is attractive, but begs the central question by incorporating an answer. Of course, it is a useful antidote to the need for preemptive certainty—as is our strategy of locating doctrines in the grammar which structures narrative accounts of personal transformation.

I find Wilfrid Cantwell Smith's programmatic suggestions in his *Towards a World Theology* helpful, as pointing to ways in which we could develop the skills required for fruitful comparative study: a seminar composed of articulate believers from distinct traditions, in which communication would be deemed to be achieved when each person could understand the other's account as one in which he or she could plausibly participate.[44] Such exercises, carried out regarding specific doctrines-cum-practices, might well be able to develop, in those participating, skills of comparative assessment. We might discover, for example, that the "distinction" of God from the world is more ably secured in a tradition which was also forced to articulate how two natures functioned in one person (Christ) than in the other two faiths which avow creation.[45] Short of such live encounters, however, one fears especially that we in the West will not be sufficiently aware of the threshold on which we stand, inquiring into our own traditions (in the spirit of "faith seeking understanding") as they now face other major religious traditions with palpable histories of holiness.

CHAPTER SIX

Beyond Optimism to Hope:
John of the Cross and Edith Stein
Responding to Charles Taylor

LET US EXPLORE the lived experience of creation and the contingency of being, calling upon participants from each Abrahamic tradition, for the mystery of free creation unites these otherwise quite disparate traditions. Each of these three traditions finds that mystery epitomized in human beings, whose privileged yet hybrid origin baffled the angels, yet also reveals—to those who can perceive it—a special divine image. For Sufi Islam, the fact that "on the day of *Alast*, the primordial revelation was placed in the human heart"[1] gives primacy to the creation of Adam: "Other creatures came by way of creation, Adam by way of love."[2] Reflecting on the biblical expression that human beings are made in God's "image and likeness," the Jewish philosophical theologian, Moses Maimonides, reinforces similar views on the primacy of human beings in God's intent in creating, though he resists regarding human beings as culminating creation in the sense that it was all created for their sake.[3] Christian thinkers link their anthropology directly to the Genesis texts on which Maimonides comments, yet identify the divine "image and likeness" in which human beings are said to be made with the Word of God "through whom the world is made" (John 1:10), incarnate as the Christ.

Even here, affinities with Sufi Islam abound, as the pre-existent Muhammad provides the paradigm for the created universe, much as the pre-existent Torah supplies the pattern for the order of the world: "The first essence to

59

receive the robe of honour of the command *kun* ['Be!'], and the first upon whom the sun of God's grace shone was the pure spirit of that master.[4] This 'pure spirit' of Muhammad had come to be known in Islamic mysticism as the Muhammadan light [*nur Muhammadi*]. . . . Not only was Muhammad the first in creation, but he was the purpose for which the universe was created."[5]

To be sure, the pre-existent Prophet is better compared with biblical Wisdom, as the "firstborn of all creation," than with the uncreated Word of God as elaborated in Christian trinitarian belief. Yet multiple affinities remain among all three Abrahamic faiths as they attempt to elaborate the insistence of their respective revelations that the origin of the universe comes by way of free creation on the part of the One.

What is at stake here? The principal implication of the teaching of free creation by the One is this. The order of the universe, which Aquinas identifies with the creator's primary intent, cannot be impersonal, even if the way it is "personal" escapes us. For if the metaphysics of free creation requires that everything that is comes forth continuously from the One bestowing existence to all, then (as Aquinas notes) the very being of each will be a being-to-the-creator (*esse ad creatorem*).[6] Existence itself will have the metaphysical valence of a relation, and since the One to whom it is in relation is paradigmatically intentional, so will the relation be.

Nevertheless, since the "emanation of all things from the very cause of being" is unlike any causal relation which we know, that relation can be asserted but never adequately articulated, since it will escape the terms of causality as we know it. In that case, where the beings so related are themselves intentional as well, emanation will elicit a complementary dynamic of return, all of which will be thoroughly intentional. And while this dynamic will also elude articulation in categories taken from creation, the fact that all is relating cannot but elicit an aura of wonder. As Aquinas puts it, creatures are suspended between two intellects—the

divine intellect bringing them into being and the created intellect seeking to understand them.[7] This very scheme demands that the founding relation outreach our articulation,
since it embodies the distinction of creator from creatures
which the unique mode of causality that is free creation requires. Moreover, realizing the presence of this founding relation that is constitutive of each thing lends an aura of mystery to every existent.[8]

It is that very aura of mystery, however, which Charles
Taylor contends has been eclipsed by "the secular age," introduced in the west by the Enlightenment, and in which
much of the world increasingly lives.[9] Let me suggest at the
outset that his immensely articulate description of the shift
in consciousness which a secular age demands, persuasive
as it is, exudes a Hegel-like presumption which may or may
not be accurate—that the transition is at once inevitable and
irreversible. Like many Hegelian tours de force, this presumption will be countered by fine-grained narratives offering a surprising denouement to the main lines of his per-
ceptive analysis.

How does he describe this crucial transition to a secular
age? Taylor's description is dialectical and multi-layered—
a conscious "polemic against what [he calls] 'subtraction
stories,'" which seek to explain modernity and secularity
"by human beings having lost, or sloughed off, or liberated themselves from certain earlier confining horizons, illusions, or limitations of knowledge."[10] Such stories foster
the positive valence in the term *enlightenment*, of course,
whereas Taylor attempts to show how "Western modernity,
including its secularity, is the fruit of new inventions, newly
constructed self-understandings and related practices and
can't be explained in terms of perennial features of human
life"[11] Rather, these novel features have "been coterminous
with the rise of a society in which for the first time in history
a purely self-sufficient humanism came to be a widely available option."[12] The result is a new set of "social imaginaries"
which effectively disembed society from cosmos, replacing
inherent hierarchies (or "sacred orders") with "the mutual

respect and mutual service of the individuals who make up society,"[13] "agents who through disengaged, disciplined action can reform their own lives, as well as the larger social order,"[14] creating a "public sphere [as] an association which is constituted by nothing outside of the common action we carry out in it: coming to a common mind, where possible, through the exchange of ideas."[15] This social imaginary, embodying the "crucial fiction of 'we, the people' . . . articulates into a new understanding of time,"[16] which is central to the understanding of secularity into which Taylor would introduce us.

He reminds us how Walter Benjamin made "'homogeneous, empty time' . . . central to modernity,"[17] which Taylor delineates as a feature of the social imaginary which has overtaken us: "Our encasing in secular time is also something we have brought about in the way we live and order our lives. It has been brought about by the same social and ideological changes which have wrought disenchantment. In particular, the disciplines of our modern civilized order have led us to measure and organize time as never before in human history. Time has become a precious resource, not to be 'wasted.' The result has been the creation of a tight, ordered time environment. This has enveloped us, until it comes to seem like nature."[18]

Benedict Anderson exploits this novel sense of time to explain "the new sense of belonging to a nation, [with] society as a whole consisting of the simultaneous happening of all the myriad events which mark the lives of its members at that moment. These events are the fillers of a kind of homogeneous time. This very clear, unambiguous concept of simultaneity belongs to an understanding of time as exclusively secular,"[19] in stark contrast to Augustine's sense of the elusive present moment imaging eternity in time, and celebrated in liturgical punctuations of continuous chronological time. Theological readers will be reminded of the way Catherine Pickstock (After Writing: On the Liturgical Consummation of Philosophy, 1998) delineates modernity's "mathematicization of time," in her persuasive argument that nothing short of incorporating the *kairos*, "acceptable time," of liturgical practice into philosophical discourse will enable it to articulate transcendence.

This persuasive description of "a uniform, univocal secular time, which we try to measure and control in order to get things done" reminds us instantly of Max Weber's "famous description of ... an iron cage. It occludes all higher times, makes them even hard to conceive."[20] Ironically, Taylor's relentlessly potent prose also tends to replace the "widely available option" in his original description of the project ("for the first time in history a purely self-sufficient humanism came to be a widely available option") with an ineluctable and encompassing "cage," reinforced by a set of "social imaginaries" without alternative.

I have identified this penchant with a Hegel-like presumption which takes the transition to be inevitable and irreversible. Much like Karl Marx's trenchant critique of capitalism in his *Economic and Philosophical Manuscripts of 1844*, Taylor's analysis can hardly be gainsaid, yet reflective persons made aware of subsisting within the "cage" may well be led to search for spiritual antidotes. Freedom knows interior responses to confining situations—much as "social imaginaries," once made explicit, can suggest hitherto hidden ways to dissolve their constraining power. But the standing contribution of Marx, and now Taylor, will be to remind us how effectively the forces at work reinforce a secular age. Here again, to learn how to articulate the constraints such an age imposes may open ways for us to feel it as constraining, and so begin to appreciate what we are missing.

Taylor himself notes "certain contemporary modes of post-modernism which deny, attack or scoff at the claims of self-sufficient reason," which he has identified as the hallmark of a secular age, yet finds "they offer no outside source for the reception of power,"[21] by which he characterizes an authentically religious outlook.[22] I would plump for a more benign variety of postmodern reflections, exemplified by John Henry Newman or Bernard Lonergan, which nudge us into a more properly medieval ethos where critical reason will have to be tempered with a conscious faith to realize its own inherent goals. Indeed, something of this sort will provide the denouement for Taylor's long journey, in the last part of the work, which elaborates "Conditions of Belief" in five stages, culminating in a set of narrated "Conversions."

As their provocative titles suggest, the stages detail fissures in the prevailing social imaginaries sustaining or resulting from a secular age: "the Immanent Frame," "Cross Pressures," "Dilemmas 1 and 2," and "the Unquiet Frontiers of Modernity." So the point of this sinuous apologetic work turns out to be an Archimedean point which will serve as the fulcrum on which a "return to self" will hinge—a reversal gaining a special poignancy as it is executed in the face of the social imaginaries which had purportedly eliminated such moves. So the "drama of atheistic humanism" (to purloin the title of Henri de Lubac's earlier tour de force) ushers in a dramatic resurgence of faith, capturing the death/resurrection motif of Taylor's own faith. And what gives the Archimedean point its leverage is what we might call "wonderment." (Since we have not called it that before).

Taylor supplies the fulcrum, ironically, in his illuminating chapters identified as "The Turning Point," where he delineates the western gutting, if not trivialization, of the Christian story (largely sanitized of its roots in Jewish sensibility) under the titles of "Providential Deism" (Ch. 6) and "Impersonal Order" (Ch. 7). It is this deliberate naturalization, if you will, of Christian tradition, abetted by its political ascendancy (whose dark underbelly Taylor curiously omits mentioning—slavery and other forms of exploitation, first in Ireland and then in Africa and Asia), which turns out to leave an increasingly manifest void where faith had offered "fullness" or "wholeness": "The narratives of modernity have been questioned, contested, attacked, since their inception in the eighteenth century. . . . Running through all these attacks is the specter of meaninglessness; that as a result of the denial of transcendence, of heroism, of deep feeling, we are left with a view of human life which is empty, cannot inspire commitment, offers nothing really worthwhile, cannot answer the craving for goals to which we can dedicate ourselves."[23] And to recall the dimension of political hegemony, we should add "self-congratulatory"; it is *we* who offer the paradigm for what is human, even while our actions toward others unlike us were hardly humane!

Yet Taylor could hardly draw such a convincing picture of the cognate movements of "Enlightenment" and "Reform" were he to regard their results as simply debilitating. In fact, he always reminds us of the capacity of these movements, with their social imaginaries, to empower human beings to achievement, especially in their struggle for human freedom—however chauvinistic that turned out to be. Yet his resolute refusal to indulge in "subtraction stories" opens him to the ambiguities latent in what he dubs the "Modern Moral Order," which he can celebrate for "its endorsing of universal human rights and welfare as one of our crucial goals . . . as our stepping some into a wider, qualitatively different sense of inter-human solidarity . . . analogous to certain precedent ones in history: inaugurated, for instance, by Buddha, by Stoicism, by the New Testament preaching ('in Christ is neither Jew nor Greek, slave or free, male or female') and by Muhammad."[24]

Yet for all that, something was felt to be missing—specifically, "the aspiration to wholeness, particularly as it emerges in the reaction to the disciplined, buffered self in the romantic period. The protest here is that the rational, disengaged agent is sacrificing something essential in realizing his ideals. What is sacrificed is often described as spontaneity or creativity, but it is even more frequently identified with our feelings, our bodily existence."[25] And if he reminds us that "this understanding of wholeness which has to include a crucial place for the body is a legacy of our Christian civilization,"[26] he also insists that restoring it to our "social imaginary" will involve re-appropriating that tradition across several baffle plates of distortion on the part of Christianity itself.[27] So if the journey to "a secular age" has even been a dialectical one, so will be the move beyond its "iron cage." Here there can be no substitute for narratives of "conversion" out of "the immanent frame." We have seen two such narratives at work—in Augustine and in Etty Hillesum. Let us now follow their yet more startling extension—in John of the Cross and in Edith Stein.[28]

Hope Beyond Our Capacity to Hope:
John of the Cross and Edith Stein

We have all been gifted with teachers and guides, companions and friends, present to us whether currently living or not, who shape our lives by giving us the courage to live and to love. The letters of Edith Stein, as daughter, student, companion, teacher, and then as Teresa Benedicta of the Cross, testify to a person replete with friends and nourished by relationships which she herself cultivated.

Responding to the initial invitation of another Teresa to collaborate in the reform of Carmel, John of the Cross devoted the bulk of his life as a religious to that work, carrying out assigned duties in the order despite acute and recriminatory opposition, yet he never allowed any of it to displace his vocation as a spiritual guide. Indeed, his two most lyrical works, *The Spiritual Canticle* and *The Living Flame of Love*, were composed at the behest of friends who had come to accompany him in the spirit: Ana de Jesús and Doña Ana de Peñalosa, respectively.

The plot thickens as Edith Stein, also called forth on the journey which led her to become Sister Teresa Benedicta by her encounter with Teresa de Avila, devotes what were to be the final months of her life attempting "to understand John of the Cross in his life and works, considering him from a point of view that enables us to envisage this unity." Occasioned by the then impending fourth centenary of John, this philosopher seized that opportunity to "penetrate to the unity" of John's life and works, incorporating "an interpretation, offering what she believes a lifetime of effort to have taught her about the laws of intellectual and spiritual being and life." So she does not hesitate to expound "her theories on spirit, faith and contemplation," specifying that "what [she says] on ego, freedom and person is not derived from the writings of our holy Father John . . . for only modern philosophy has set itself the task of working out a philosophy of the person such as is suggested in the passages just mentioned."[29]

This relationship of master to disciple, sustained by the family of Carmel extended over space and time, allows the apprentice to exercise her own experience coupled to philosophical developments achieved in the intervening four centuries. So the relationship between these two—a poet with an exquisite grasp of matters in philosophical theology, and a vigorous philosopher brought through her interior life to a refined sensibility for the poetics of love—can epitomize our thesis about the fruitfulness of lives lived in so rich a community of prayer and inquiry.

In attempting an appreciation of the homage of this philosophical spirit to her poetic guide and predecessor in Carmel, I shall utilize a work completed a few years before—*Finite and Eternal Being: Attempting an Ascent to the Meaning of Being*, which followed her self-imposed task of appropriating the thought of Thomas Aquinas by translating his *Disputed Questions on Truth*. The later synthetic work on the metaphysics of Aquinas owes an express gratitude to Erich Przywara's *Analogia Entis*, a work which presaged the fruitful efforts of Louis Geiger and Cornelius Fabro to call attention to the centrality of participation in the metaphysics of Thomas Aquinas.

What is remarkable about Edith Stein's inquiry is her ability to penetrate to the heart of Aquinas's subtle and elusive discourse on being, and to do so without the benefit of the studies cited—indeed, without much reliance on secondary literature at all. Yet her own confessed formation in "the school of Edmund Husserl . . . and phenomenological method" may have offered her a prescient optic for the potencies of Aquinas's language in trying to bring to expression this axial notion of metaphysics which in fact resists any proper conceptual formation.[30]

But let us first try to evoke the rich person of this scholar who found herself so drawn by truth as it was unveiled to her, as well as drawn to those with whom she shared this adventure: friends and students (who quickly became friends). Gifted with a thoroughly intellectual temperament, her advice to a colleague, Fritz Kaufmann, reveals as well just how centered she already was at 28 (in 1919): "I am worried at seeing how, for months, you have avoided doing purely philosophical work, and am gradually beginning to wonder whether your 'profession' should not lie in a different direction. Please do not take this as a vote of 'no confidence' or as doubting your ability. I only mean that one should not use force to make the center of one's life anything that fails to give one the right kind of satisfaction."[31]

Equally drawn as she was to scholarship and to guiding others to cognate goals, she could be utterly forthright in critique of another's work, as evidenced in her response to Maria Bruck's dissertation comparing two German philosophers: "I am convinced that if you have an opportunity to work for a few years longer at systematic philosophy, you will yourself experience the need to go beyond [this work]; not merely take an independent position on the problems you have touched but, above all, to tackle the interpretation from the basis of clearly established final principles. Without that, no actual comparison of what is meant as systematic philosophy is possible. From the start I missed a sharp delineation of what Brentano and Husserl understood as the real and as essence, and several other matters."[32]

To be sure, this communication begins gently: "Undoubtedly this work demanded a great deal of effort from you. It is very neat and conscientious and will surely be of lasting use for anyone who will study the relationship of Husserl to Brentano," but its author cannot have failed to discern, in her friend Edith's words, that she had rather missed the point—philosophically.

In a more personal vein, to a former student who was herself discerning a vocation to religious life, Edith writes,

> God leads each of us on an individual way; one reaches the goal more easily and more quickly than another. We can do very little ourselves, compared to what is done to us. But that little bit we must do. Primarily, this consists before all else of persevering in prayer to find the right way, and of following without resistance the attraction of grace when we feel it. Whoever acts in this way and perseveres patiently will not be able to say that his efforts were in vain. But one may not set a deadline for the Lord. . . . Among the books you got as a child, do you have Andersen's Fairy Tales? If so, read the story of the ugly duckling. I believe in your swan-destiny.[33]

And to another former student, now teaching in school, also discerning religious life, she writes,

> To contend for souls and love them in the Lord is the Christian's duty and, actually, a special goal of the Dominican Order. But if that is your goal and if the thought of marriage is farthest from your mind, then it will be good if you soon begin to wear appropriate dress. That will make it clear to people who it is they are dealing with. Otherwise there will be the danger of your misleading others, of your behavior being misinterpreted (I would be surprised if, without your being aware of it, that has not already happened at times), and your achieving exactly the opposite of what you desire.[34]

It should be clear how those who associated with this woman could be assured of hearing the truth as she saw it, yet at the same time many seemed ineluctably drawn to her, as she reminds her colleague Fritz (in 1931), "The circle of persons whom I consider as connected with me has increased so much in the course of the years that it is entirely impossible to keep in touch by the usual means. But I have other ways and means of keeping the bonds alive."[35]

Edith had, early on, been thwarted from pursuing her second doctorate [*Habilitationschrift*] for the simple reason that she was a woman, and her remarks (again to Fritz Kaufmann) on the academic politics surrounding the matter are unyielding.[36] Yet within two weeks, she finds herself consoling him: "It was terribly dear of you to be so zealous on my behalf, but I must tell you that things have gone very well for me in the past weeks and that I am no longer the least bit furious or sad. Instead I find the whole matter very funny. After all, I do not consider life on the whole to carry so much weight that it would matter a great deal what position I occupy. And I would like you to make that attitude your own."[37]

She realized perfectly well that she would never be admitted to university teaching without the second doctorate, yet service was already more important than a career, so, soon after her baptism on 1 January 1922 (at the age of 31), she immersed herself in secondary teaching at a Dominican Sisters' school in Speyer (Bavaria)—a position she held for nine years until she resigned to complete her translation of Aquinas. All during this time, she immersed herself in lectures on the place of women, especially in Catholic circles, remarking in 1931, "During my years in the Gymnasium and as a young student [at the university] I was a radical feminist. Then I lost interest in the whole question. Now, because I am obliged to do so, I seek purely objective solutions."[38]

Fully engaged in teaching young women, she made their concerns her own, yet in a quite disinterested way. This vocational commitment was, if anything, intensified in her next post at the *Deutsches Institut für Wissenschaftliche Pädagogik* (German Institute for Scientific Pedagogy), where she continued to lecture on women's issues until 1933 when the National Socialists insisted that Jews be deprived of teaching posts. Writing again to Fritz Kaufmann, she was able to say, "The *umsturz* was for me a sign from heaven that I might now go the way that I had long considered as mine. After a final visit with my relatives in Breslau and a difficult farewell from my dear mother, I entered the monastery of the Carmelite nuns here last Saturday and thus became a daughter of St. Teresa, who earlier inspired me to conversion."[39] In that life, she would be able to pursue her interior vocation intellectually as well, and be prepared for the ultimate test, to come in less than a decade.

From what we have seen of Edith Stein, we would be hard-pressed to read her move to Carmel as "leaving the world," but rather as intensifying her presence to a world gone mad. Indeed, her letters from Breslau to her friends, on the cusp of entering Carmel, invite them all to visit her there, while reflections in an earlier (1928) letter to a Dominican sister friend help us to read the move more accurately:

> Immediately before, and for a good while after my conversion, I was of the opinion that to lead a religious life meant one had to give up all that was secular and to live totally immersed in thoughts of the Divine. But gradually I realized that something else is asked of us in this world and that, even in the contemplative life, one may not sever the connection with the world. I even believe that the deeper one is drawn into God, the more one must "go out of oneself": that is, one must go to the world in order to carry the divine life into it. The only essential is that one finds, first of all, a quiet corner in which one can communicate with God as though there were nothing else, and that must be done daily. . . . Furthermore, [it is essential] that one accept one's particular mission there, preferably for each day, and not make one's own choice. Finally, one is to consider oneself totally as an instrument, especially with regard to the abilities one uses to perform one's special tasks, in our case, e.g., intellectual ones. We are to see them as something used, not by us, but by God in us. . . . My life begins anew each morning, and ends every evening; I have neither plans nor prospects beyond it.[40]

As we shall see, it would be difficult to find a better formula for describing a life patterned on the transformation outlined by John of the Cross; Edith seemed to have been prepared to move quite naturally into Sister Teresa Benedicta of the Cross.

While she did not complete her constructive monograph on the unity of John's life and work until her final days, we can easily discern her pull to Carmel, first in her attraction to Teresa of Avila, and then in her inner affinity for the purity of John of the Cross's presentation of the inner dynamics of a life of faith. John is disarmingly forthright in identifying the goal of that journey ("the union and transformation of the [person] in God")[41] as well as the means ("faith alone, which is the only proximate and proportionate means to union with God").[42] He is at pains to distinguish this intentional union from the "union between God and creatures [which] always exists [by which] God sustains every soul and dwells in it substantially. . . . By it, He conserves their being so that if the union would end they would immediately be annihilated and cease to exist."[43]

So John will presume the unique metaphysical relation of all creatures to their source which Meister Eckhart elaborated from Aquinas's "distinction," and does not hesitate to call it a union—indeed, an "essential or substantial union." This grounding fact attends all creatures, hence it is natural and found in everything (though displayed differently in animate and inanimate—and in animate, differs from animals to humans, though among humans it can still be found in "the greatest sinner in the world"), while the intentional union is supernatural and can only be found "where there is a likeness of love [such that] God's will and the [person's] are in conformity."[44]

We shall see that what eliminates any prospect of heteronomy between those two wills is precisely this "non-reciprocal relation of dependence" which attends all creatures. But let us attend first to the internal connection between faith and union which John confidently asserts. What makes this sound so startling is our propensity to confine such talk to mystics, while reducing faith to belief (holding certain propositions to be true). This is a long and complex debate in Christian theology, which often cuts oddly across confessional lines, so the best we can do here is to remind ourselves that John of the Cross could well have been responding from the Iberian Peninsula to sixteenth-century winds from northern Europe. He did so by elaborating some key assertions of Aquinas to cut through the debates which polarized intellect and will in the act of faith.

First, here is Aquinas: "Faith is a sort of knowledge [*cognitio quaedam*] in that it makes the mind assent to something. The assent is not due to what is seen by the believer but to what is seen by him who is believed."[45] The one who is believed is, of course, the Word of God incarnate, Jesus, as mediated through the scriptures. Therefore, this peculiar "sort of knowledge" is rooted in an interpersonal relation of the believer with Jesus.

It is that relation, at the root of faith, which John of the Cross sets out to explore, quite aware that what results from it will "fall short of the mode of knowing [*cognitio*] which is properly called knowledge [*scientia*], for such knowledge causes the mind to assent through what is seen and through an understanding of first principles."[46] More positively, Aquinas characterizes faith as "an act of mental assent commanded by the will, [so] to believe perfectly our mind must tend unfailingly towards the perfection of truth, in unfailing service of that ultimate goal for the sake of which our will is commanding our mind's assent."[47] Unlike ordinary belief, then, faith must be an act of the whole person, involving a personal and critical quest for a truth which outreaches our proper expression. John focuses critically on our concepts: "Nothing which could possibly be imagined or comprehended in this life can be a proximate means of union with God,"[48] since "nothing created or imagined can serve the intellect as a proper means for union with God; all that can be grasped by the intellect would serve as an obstacle rather than a means, if a person were to become attached to it."[49]

Following Aquinas's lead, we must be able to let our conceptualities "lead us on by the hand" (*manuductio*), as John does, to a goal which transcends them. That goal, we recall, is "union and transformation of the [person] in God," already intimated in the sort of faith which Thomas and John envisage. As Augustine had already worked it out, Christian faith differs from ordinary belief in being a response to an utterly gratuitous invitation, which could never be initiated by persons themselves.

This treatment of faith and union anticipates the critiques of both Freud and Marx, while leaving room for both. Though Freud would belittle religious faith as projections, Aquinas does not hesitate to say that "faith that does not rely on divine truth can fail and believe falsehood."[50] If, however, we regard John of the Cross as developing Aquinas's lapidary exposition of faith, authentic faith will ever involve a journey of responding rather than initiating, with distracting projections facing a searing critique. With regard to Marx, it is John's forthright insistence on union which responds to Marx's characterization of Christian faith as alienating human beings from their authentic life and work by offering a distracting "heavenly reward"—for the union of which John speaks begins now.

Yet Marx's account may well address a Christian ethos quite innocent of the tradition John articulates: an internal connection between faith and union. So Marx's critique can well inspire the kind of internal critique which John's account of faith demands. Indeed, the demands of that journey of faith which John outlines are utterly rigorous: "We shall explain how in order to journey to God the intellect must be perfected in the darkness of faith, the memory in the emptiness of hope, and the will in the nakedness and absence of every affection [unrelated to the goal of union]."[51]

A poetic characterization of that intentional union is offered in his "Living Flame of Love," where we can cite the initial stanza of the poem together with statements from his own commentary.

> O living flame of love
> That tenderly wounds my soul

In its deepest center! Since
Now You are not oppressive,
Now Consummate! If it be your will:
Tear through the veil of this sweet encounter!

The commentary begins,

The soul now feels that it is all inflamed in the divine
union . . . and that in the most intimate part of its substance it is flooded with no less than rivers of glory,
abounding in delights, and that from its bosom flow
rivers of living waters [John 7:38], which the Son of
God declared will rise up in such souls. According-
ly it seems, because it is so vigorously transformed
in God, so sublimely possessed by Him, and arrayed
with such rich gifts and virtues, that it is singularly
close to beatitude—so close that only a thin veil sep-
arates it.[52]
This flame of love is the Spirit of the Bridegroom,
which is the Holy Spirit. . . . Such is the activity of the
Holy Spirit in the soul transformed in love: the interi-
or acts He produces shoot up flames for they are acts
of inflamed love, in which the will of the soul united with that flame, made one with it, loves most sublimely. . . . Thus in this state the soul cannot make acts
because the Holy Spirit makes them all and moves it
towards them. As a result all the acts of the soul are
divine, since the movement toward these acts and
their execution stems from God. Hence it seems to a
person that every time this flame shoots up, making
him love with delight and divine quality, it is giving
him eternal life, since it raises him up to the activity
of God in God.[53]

There is no hint of heteronomy here, I would suggest,
because John presumes that unique metaphysical relation of
person (soul) to its source which Meister Eckhart develops
from Aquinas.
Sister Teresa Benedicta had become attuned to that
unique relation of creatures to their creator in her study of

Aquinas on eternal and temporal being, which led her into the presence of "the great mystery of creation: that God has called forth each being into its differentiated being; a manifold of beings in which what is one in God is there separate. . . . [Yet] the subsistence of creatures is no longer that of a portrait over against the one portrayed, or of a work over against the artist doing it. Earlier [thinkers] had likened the relation to that of a mirror to the object in the mirror, or of refracted light to its pure source, yet these remain but imperfect images for what is quite incomparable."[54]

She then goes on to compare the creator/creature relation to the relations among the divine persons:

> The entire divine essence is common to all three persons. So what remains is simply the differences of the persons as such: a perfect unity of *we*, which no community of finite persons could ever realize, yet in this unity the difference of *I* from *you* remains, without which no *we* is possible. . . . Indeed, the *we* as the unity of *I* and *you*—"I and the Father are one" (John 10:30)—is a higher unity than the *I*. For in its most perfect sense, it is the unity of love. Now love as assent to a good is possible as the self-love of an *I*, but love is more than such an assent, more than a "valuing." It is gift of oneself to the *thou*, and in its perfection—on the strength of manifold gifts of self—an existential unity [*Einssein*]. Since God is love, divine being must be an existential unity of a multiplicity of persons, while the divine name "I am" is identical in meaning with "I give myself totally to you," "I am one with a *you*," and so also identical with "we are." The love of the life interior to God can never be replaced, however, by the love between God and creatures, which can never attain love in its highest perfection— even when it be realized in the richest perfection of glory. For the highest love is differentiated eternal love: God loves creatures from eternity, whereas God can never be loved by them from eternity.[55]

So while the *we* of human lovers may offer an image for divine triunity, it will always fall short of that eternal unity. Yet, since the relation of creatures to creator also defies representation, the unity with God to which humans can be elevated by grace may be likened to that within the triune God, even though the one can never replace the other. What is incomparable can nonetheless be compared! That is the paradox into which the analogical metaphysics of Aquinas invites us, and to which the poetic genius of John of the Cross will give its most proper expression. For his poetry gives voice to the utterly unique distinction of creatures from creator, which we have seen John already calling a union in the nature of created things with their creator, and one which becomes intentionally so in those who permit the interior transformation by the Holy Spirit into "images of god" become "images of Christ." In this way the circumincession of human and divine which characterizes Jesus can be bestowed upon human agents who have been turned into lovers.

So did Edith Stein—become Sister Teresa Benedicta of the Cross—trace the divine becoming so aptly described by John of the Cross in her life and works, as he had limned it in his, that her apprenticeship to him reflects ours to them both, in the circumincession of emulation which characterizes a community of revelation, as friendships sustain each of us in our search for Truth as we attempt to incorporate that Truth into the truth of our lives.

NOTES

PREFACE

1. See the response of Muslim intellectuals to Pope Benedict XVI, "A Common Word between Us," http://www.acommonword.com.

2. Official sources for Catholic social teaching can be found in David O'Brien and Thomas Shannon, eds., *Catholic Social Thought: The Documentary Heritage* (Maryknoll, NY: Orbis, 1992), with commentaries and interpretations in Kenneth Himes, OFM, et al., eds., *Modern Catholic Social Teaching* (Washington, DC: Georgetown University Press, 2004), and topically arranged: *Compendium of he Social Doctrine of the Church* [Pontifical Council for Justice and Peace] ((Washington, DC: United States Conference of Catholic Bishops, 2005), and by titles on the Vatican website.

3. See the multiple works of Susan George, notably *The Lugano Report: On Preserving Capitalism in the Twenty-First Century* (London: Pluto, 2003).

INTRODUCTION

1. Bernard J. F. Lonergan, *Insight* (London: Longmans, 1957); René Girard, *Des choses cachées depuis la fondation du monde* (Paris: Grasset, 1981) English translation—*Things Hidden from the Foundation of the World* (Palo Alto, CA: Stanford University Press, 1987).

2. Avital Wohlman, *Eros and Logos: The Conflict between Isocrates and Plato on the Subject of Athenian Culture As Seen through the Symposium* (Jerusalem: Kesset, 1993).

3. Frederick E. Crowe, "Complacency and Concern in the Thought of St. Thomas," in *Three Thomist Studies*, ed. Fred Lawrence [Lonergan Workshop supplementary volume 16] (Chesnut Hill, MA: Boston College, 2000).

4. Pierre Hadot, *Philosophy as a Way of Life: Spiritual Exercises from Socrates to Foucault*, essays edited by Arnold Davidson (Chicago, IL: University of Chicago Press, 1995).

5. Eleonore Stump, "Intellect, Will, and the Principle of Alternate Possibilities," in John Martin Fischer, ed., *Perspectives on Moral Responsibility* (Ithaca, NY: Cornell University Press, 1993), amplified in her recent *Aquinas* (New York: Routledge, 2002), Ch. 9: "Freedom: Action, Intellect and Will."

6. See Kenneth Sayre in Frederick J. Crosson and Kenneth M. Sayre, eds., *Philosophy and Cybernetics: Essays Delivered to the Philosophic Institute for Artificial Intelligence at the University of Notre Dame* (Notre Dame, IN: University of Notre Dame Press, 1967).

7. Lewis Carroll, *Alice in Wonderland* and *Through the Looking Glass* (New York: Schocken, 1978).

CHAPTER ONE

1. For a clear and cogent such account, see Peter Van Inwagen, *An Essay on Free Will* (Oxford: Oxford University Press, 1983).

2. See her critical exploration, Eleonore Stump "Intellect, Will, and the Principle of Alternate Possibilities," in John Martin Fischer, ed., *Perspectives on Moral Responsibility* (Ithaca, NY: Cornell University Press, 1993), amplified in Brian Davies, ed., *Thomas Aquinas: Contemporary Philosophical Perspectives* (Oxford: Oxford University Press, 2002) 275–94; and in her recent *Aquinas* (New York: Routledge, 2002), Ch. 9: "Freedom: Action, Intellect and Will."

3. This is the burden of my *Knowing the Unknowable God: Ibn-Sina, Maimonides, Aquinas* (Notre Dame, IN: University of Notre Dame Press, 1986).

4. Josef Pieper, *The Silence of St. Thomas: Three Essays* (New York: Pantheon, 1957): "The Negative Element in the Philosophy of St. Thomas," 47–67; re-issued: South Bend, IN: St. Augustine's, 2002.

5. For a far more nuanced version of this transition, see Charles Taylor, *A Secular Age* (Cambridge, MA: Belknap Press of Harvard University Press, 2007).

6. The classic Gadamer text is *Truth and Method*, English translation by Joel Weinsheimer and Donald Marshall of *Wahrheit und Methode* (New York: Continuum 1997); for an imaginative use of his central point, see Roxanne Euben, *Enemy in the Mirror* (Princeton, NJ: Princeton University Press, 1999).

7. Consult preferably Nicholas Lash's edition of Henry Newman, *An Essay in Aid of a Grammar of Assent* (Notre Dame, IN: University of Notre Dame Press, 1979) for its illuminating introduction, yet also note the way in which Joseph Dunne utilizes Newman to initiate his recovery of Aristotle's *phronesis* in his *Back to the Rough Ground* (Notre Dame, IN: University of Notre Dame Press, 1993).

8. Published in Gary Watson, ed., Free Will (New York: Oxford University Press, 1982) as "Human Freedom and the Self," 24–35, citation at 26.

9. Alasdair MacIntyre, *Dependent Rational Animals* (London: Duckworth, 1999).

10. See note 2 for Stump reference; Mary Clark's "Willing Freely According to Thomas Aquinas" is published in Arthur Hyman's festschrift, *A Straight Path: Essays in Honor of Arthur Hyman,* eds. Ruth Link-Salinger, Jeremiah Hackett, et al. (Washington, DC: Catholic University of America Press,1988), 49–56.

11. See my *Freedom and Creation in Three Traditions* (Notre Dame, IN: University of Notre Dame Press, 1994), 157–59: "The Surd of Sin."

12. See Hugh McCann, "Divine Sovereignty and the Freedom of the Will," *Faith and Philosophy* 12 (1995) 582–98, as well as his "The Author of Sin,"

Faith and Philosophy 22 (2005): 144–59; and my *Freedom and Creation in Three Traditions* (Notre Dame, IN: University of Notre Dame Press, 1994) Ch. 7: "On the Relation between the Two Actors," 95–140.

13. See John Garvey's constructive essay in legal philosophy: *What are Freedoms For?* (Cambridge, MA: Harvard University Press, 2001).

CHAPTER TWO

1. Among others, see Bonnie Kent, *Virtues of the Will: The Transformation of Ethics in the Late Thirteenth Century* (Washington, DC: Catholic University of America Press, 1995).

2. On the condemnations of 1277, see Roland Hissette, *Enquete sur les 219 articles condamnes a Paris le 7 mars 1277* (Louvain: Publications Universitaires, 1977); as well as the more general discussion by J. M. M. H. Thijsen, *Censure and Heresy at the University of Paris 1200–1400* (Philadelphia: University of Pennsylvania Press, 1998).

3. See my "Creation, Will and Knowledge in Aquinas and Duns Scotus," *Pragmatik I* (Hamburg: Felix Meiner, 1986) 246–57; reprinted in my *Faith and Freedom* (Oxford: Blackwell, 2004), Ch. 12.

4. For the Mu'tazilite strategies, see my *Freedom and Creation in Three Traditions* (Notre Dame, IN: University of Notre Dame Press), 51–52, 77–79.

5. On what is called the Ash'arite (or orthodox) teaching, see Daniel Gimaret, *La Doctrine d'al Ash'ari* (Paris: Cerf, 1990), as well as my *Freedom and Creation*.

6. Brian Davies's summary description of this "school" makes this point in a telling way: "It is false, we are told, that God is incomprehensible. He is, in fact, something very familiar. He is a person. And he has properties in common with other persons. He changes, he learns, and is acted on. He also has beliefs, which alter with the changes in the objects of his beliefs. And he is by no means the source of all that is real in the universe. He is not, for example, the cause of my free actions. These come from me, not from God. He permits them, but they stand to him as an observed item stands to an observer. He is not their maker. He is only their enabler." ("Letter from America," *New Blackfriars* 84 (2003): 377).

7. See my "Creation, Metaphysics, and Ethics," *Faith and Philosophy* 18 (2001): 204–21.

8. This is what Robert Sokolowski has denominated "the distinction" in his seminal *God of Faith and Reason* (Washington, DC: Catholic University of America Press, 1993).

9. See my "Aquinas's Appropriation of *Liber de causis* to Articulate the Creator as Cause-of-Being," in Fergus Kerr, ed., *Contemplating Aquinas* (London: SCM Press, 2003), 55–74.

10. See my "Essence Avicenna and Greek Philosophy," MIDEO (*Melanges Institut Dominicain d'Etudes Orientales* (Cairo)) 17 (1986): 53–66.

11. For an astute analysis of the tradition of participation, see Rudi te Velde, *Participation and Substantiality in Thomas Aquinas* (Leiden: Brill, 1996).

12. Søren Kierkegaard, as Anti-Climacus, enjoying parrying with "Socrates" over the presence and execution of evil actions, in his *Sickness unto Death*, tr. and ed., Howard and Edna Hong (Princeton, NJ: Princeton University Press, 1980).

13. Genesis 3 is more explicit about the temptation to "be like god" (Genesis 3), whereas the Qur'an is more clear about the original covenant (3:80–83).

14. *Summa Theologiae* 1.49.3.5. The question addresses one of Aquinas's prevailing concerns: the Manichean contention that "there is one supreme evil which is the cause of all evil." In reply to the fifth objection, which presumes that evil has the upper hand (*ut in pluribus*) in the universe, Aquinas notes that defects in natural processes are minimal, whereas "in human affairs evil appears to prevail," offering as the reason that "most human beings follow sense rather than reason"—that is, they are intent on their gratification.

15. *Tractates on the First Epistle of John*, tr. John Rettig (Washington, DC: Catholic University of America Press, 1995) 4.6, p. 179 [=Fathers of the Church, vol. 92].

16. For a fascinating parallel with Ghazali, see my translation of his *Book of Faith in Divine Unity and Trust in Divine Providence* (Louisville, KY: Fons Vitae, 2002), Introduction.

17. I have been aided in these matters by the astute investigation by D. C. Schindler, "Freedom beyond our Choosing: Augustine on the Will and its Objects," *Communio* 29 (2002): 618–53.

18. Saint Augustine, *Confessions*, trans. R. S. Pine-Coffin (Baltimore: Penguin, 1961), 8.29.

19. See Barry Miller's treatment of this issue in *The Fullness of Being: A New Paradigm for Existence* (Notre Dame, IN: University of Notre Dame Press, 2002), by contrast with Christopher Hughes, *On a Complex Theory of a Simple God: An Investigation in Aquinas' Philosophical Theology* (Ithaca, NY: Cornell University Press, 1989), 27.

CHAPTER THREE

1. David Burrell, *Knowing the Unknowable God: Ibn-Sina, Maimonides, Aquinas* (Notre Dame: University of Notre Dame Press, 1986).

2. See my *Deconstructing Theodicy* (Grand Rapids, MI: Brazos, 2008).

3. See my *Friendship and Ways to Truth* (Notre Dame, IN: University of Notre Dame Press, 2000).

4. See Terry Eagleton's review of *The God Delusion* by Richard Dawkins, in *London Review of Books* 28: 20 (19 October 2006). For a 'full blown' account, see *Reason, Faith and Revolution* (New Haven, CT: Yale University Press, 2009).

5. Charles Taylor, *A Secular Age* (Cambridge, MA: Belknap Press of Harvard University Press, 2007).

6. Roxanne Euben, *Enemy in the Mirror: Islamic Fundamentalism and the Limits of Modern Rationalism* (Princeton, NJ: Princeton University Press, 1999).

7. Herbert Fingarette, *Self-Deception* (London: Routledge, 1969).

8. See Robert Sokolowski, *God of Faith and Reason* (Washington, DC: Catholic University of America Press, 1993) with my commentary: "The Christian Distinction Celebrated and Expanded," in John Drummond and James Hart, eds., *The Truthful and the Good* (Dordrecht: Kluwer Academic, 1996), 191–206.

9. John Milbank, "Only Theology Overcomes Metaphysics," in *The Word Made Strange* (Oxford: Blackwell, 1997), 7–35.

CHAPTER FOUR

1. George Steiner, *Real Presences* (London: Faber and Faber, 1989).

2. Dorothy L. Sayers, *The Mind of the Maker*, ed. by Susan Howatch (London: Continuum International, 2004).

3. Portions of the following have been adapted from my "Act of Creation with its Theological Consequences," in Thomas Weinandy, Daniel Keating, John Yocum, eds., *Aquinas on Doctrine: A Critical Introduction* (London: T & T Clark, 2004), 27–44.

4. See my *Knowing the Unknowable God: Ibn-Sina, Maimonides, Aquinas* (Notre Dame, IN: University of Notre Dame Press, 1986).

5. Saint Thomas Aquinas, *Summa Theologiae*, I, 44, 1.

6. Ibid., I, 3, 5.

7. Ibid., I, 3, 4.

8. Ibid., I, 44, 1, ad. 2.

9. Ibid., I, 13, 11; I, 3, 4; I, 45, 5; I, 45, 1; I, 45, 4, ad. 1.

10. Ibid., I, 45, 5.

11. Ibid., I, 45, 2, ad. 2.

12. Ibid., I, 19, 4, ad. 4.

13. Ibid., I, 32, 1, ad. 3.

14. Ibid., I, 14, 8, esp. ad. 3.

15. Ibid., I, 14, 11. See also my extended treatment of these issues in *Freedom and Creation in Three Traditions* (Notre Dame, IN: University of Notre Dame Press, 1993) 105–19.

16. Aquinas, *Summa Theologiae*, I, 45, 3.

17. Ibid., I, 3, 8.

18. See Sara Grant's comparative study of Aquinas and Shankara for this creative proposal to find a positive way to express the relation attendant upon "the distinction": *Towards an Alternative Theology: Confessions of a Non-dualist Christian*, ed. Bradley Malkovsky (Notre Dame, IN: University of Notre Dame Press, 2002).

19. James Ross, "Creation II," in Alfred Freddoso (ed.), *The Existence and Nature of God* (Notre Dame, IN: University of Notre Dame Press, 1983), 115–41, at 128.

20. This is the burden of my *Freedom and Creation*, note 4.

21. Aquinas, *Summa Theologiae*, I, 45, 5.

22. Ibid., I, 49, 2.

23. Ibid., I, 44, 1.

24. Ibid., I, 49, 3, obj. 5; I, 48–49.

25. Ibid., I, 49, 3, ad. 5.

26. Ibid., I –II, 77 and 85.

27. Josef Pieper, "The Negative Element in the Philosophy of St. Thomas," in his *The Silence of Saint Thomas* (New York: Pantheon, 1957), 47–67.

28. See my "Theology and Philosophy" in Gareth Jones (ed.), *Blackwell Companion to Modern Theology* (Oxford: Blackwell, 2002), 34–46.

29. Rudi A. te Velde, *Participation and Substantiality in Thomas Aquinas* (Leiden: Brill, 1995).

30. Ibid., 14, 17.

31. Ibid., 18, 20.

32. Ibid., 58.

33. Ibid., 210.

34. Ibid., 211.

35. Ibid., 282–83.

36. Sara Grant, *Towards an Alternative Theology* (Notre Dame, IN: University of Notre Dame Press, 2001).

37. Aquinas, *Summa Theologiae*, I, 45, 3.

38. See my exchange with Tom Flint in *Freedom and Creation in Three Traditions* (Notre Dame, IN: University of Notre Dame Press, 1993) 112, esp. note 33.

39. Kathryn Tanner develops a sense of transcendence that is expressly "non-contrastive," illustrating that suggestive category through the history of some key questions in philosophical theology, in her *God and Creation in Christian Theology* (Oxford: Blackwell, 1988).

40. Aquinas, *Summa Theologiae*, I, 45, 1.

41. See my *Knowing the Unknowable God* (Notre Dame, IN: University of Notre Dame Press, 1987) 86–91.

42. As in William Hasker's treatment of the issues in his *God, Time, and Knowledge* (Ithaca, NY: Cornell University Press, 1989).

43. Harm Goris, *Free Creatures of an Eternal God* (Leuven: Peeters, 1996).

CHAPTER FIVE

1. Portions of the following have been adapted from my *Faith and Freedom: An Interfaith Perspective* (Oxford: Blackwell, 2004), Ch. 16.

2. Saint Augustine, *Confessions*, trans. R. S. Pine-Coffin (Baltimore: Penguin, 1961), 1.1.

3. The relation with his long-term mistress is notoriously more problematic. His most inadvertent, and so most authentic, confession may be the indirect discourse he employs to relate how "the woman with whom I had been living was torn from my side as an obstacle to my marriage." Although he goes on to acknowledge that "this was a blow which crushed my heart to bleeding, because I loved her dearly" (6.15), does the initial "was torn" represent our usual ruse to avoid responsibility in the matter?

4. I am indebted to an unpublished study by my colleague Frederick J. Crosson: "Cicero and Augustine," delivered at a colloquium at Notre Dame, 1985.

5. One is reminded of the thesis developed by Patrick Sherry in *Spirits, Saints, and Immortality* (London: Macmillan, 1984): "The *absence* of such holy people over time could put a community's claims to question."

6. On the character of "the Platonists" whom Augustine mentions, and their role in his itinerary, see the chapter so titled in Peter Brown, *Augustine of Hippo* (Berkeley: University of California Press, 1968).

7. Saint Augustine, *Confessions*, 9.10.

8. Ibid., 10.6.

9. Etty Hillesum, *An Interrupted Life* (New York: Simon and Schuster, 1985), and *Letters from Westerbork* (New York: Pantheon, 1987); now combined in a single edition (New York: Henry Holt, 1996).

10. Etty Hillesum, *An Interrupted Life* and *Letters from Westerbork* (New York: Henry Holt, 1996), 76.

11. Ibid., 247.

12. Ibid., 139.

13. Ibid., 146.

14. Ibid., 249.

15. Ibid., 1.

16. Ibid., 1–82.

17. Ibid.

18. Ibid., 160–243.

19. Ibid., 160.

20. Ibid., 209–10.

21. Ibid., 91.

22. Ibid., 138.

23. Ibid., 151.

24. Ibid., 157.

25. Ibid., 89.

26. Ibid., 100–101.

27. Ibid., 186–87.

28. Ibid., 251.

29. Ibid., 255.

30. Ibid., 245.

31. Ibid., 1.

32. Ibid., 2.

33. Ibid., 241.

34. Ibid., 238.

35. Ibid., 222–23.

36. It is illustrative to observe the use to which Marc Ellis puts these diaries in his *Toward a Jewish Theology of Liberation* (Maryknoll, NY: Orbis, 1987), 96–102. For an illuminating account of convictions, see James McClendon and James Smith, *Understanding Religious Convictions* (Notre Dame, IN: University of Notre Dame Press, 1975).

37. A synoptic exploration of this sense of doctrine has been fruitfully carried out by George Lindbeck in his *Nature of Doctrine* (Philadelphia, PA: Westminster, 1985).

38. See James Ross, *Portraying Analogy* (Cambridge: Cambridge University Press, 1982), and for the history of these matters my *Analogy and Philosophical Language* (New Haven, CT: Yale University Press, 1973), as well as my "Argument in Theology: Analogy and Narrative," in Carl A. Raschke, ed., *New Dimensions in Philosophical Theology* (JAAR Thematic Studies 49/1, 1982), 37–52.

39. Karl Rahner, "Towards a Fundamental Interpretation of Vatican II," *Theological Studies* 40 (1979): 716–27.

40. John Henry Newman, *An Essay in Aid of a Grammar of Assent* (Notre Dame, IN: University of Notre Dame Press, 1979), with excellent introduction by Nicholas Lash.

41. See my *Knowing the Unknowable God: Ibn-Sina, Maimonides, and Aquinas* (Notre Dame, IN: University of Notre Dame Press, 1986), as well as "Aquinas and Maimonides: A Conversation about Proper Speech," *Immanuel* 16 (1983): 70–83.

42. See Herbert McCabe's appendix, "Signifying Imperfectly," in *Summa Theologiae* 1.12–13 (*Knowing and Naming God*) (New York: McGraw-Hill, 1964).

43. C. G. Jung, *Psychology of the Transference* (Princeton, NJ: Princeton University Press, 1966), 30.

44. Wilfred Cantwell Smith, *Towards a World Theology* (Philadelphia, PA: Westminster, 1981), 98–101.

45. Robert Sokolowski develops this point in his *The God of Faith and Reason* (Notre Dame, IN: University of Notre Dame Press, 1982/Washington, D.C.: Catholic University of America Press, 1995), 31–40.

CHAPTER SIX

1. From Annabel Keeler, *Sufi Hermeneutics: The Qur'an Commentary of Rashid al-Din Maybudi* (Oxford: Oxford University Press, 2006; and London: Institute of Ismaili Studies, 2006), 139: Maybudi, *Kashf* III, p. 571; see also *Kashf* VIII, p. 545, where Maybudi states that human beings alone among creatures are privileged with the "look of love" from God (Keeler, 146, n. 54).

2. Georges Anawati and Louis Gardet, *La mystique musulmane* (Paris: Vrin, 1961), 131.

3. Moses Maimonides, *Guide of the Perplexed* (New York: Dover, 1956; Chicago: University of Chicago Press, 1963), 3.13.

4. *Kashf* IX, p. 375 (Keeler, *Sufi Hermeneutics*, 130, 145, n.36).

5. Keeler, *Sufi Hermeneutics*, 130.

6. Saint Thomas Aquinas, *Summa Theologiae*, I, 45, 3.

7. Ibid., I, 14, 8, 3.

8. See Robert Sokolowski, *God of Faith and Reason* (Notre Dame, IN:

University of Notre Dame Press, 1982 / Washington, DC: Catholic University of America Press, 1995).

9. Charles Taylor, *A Secular Age* (Cambridge, MA: Belknap Press of Harvard University Press, 2007).

10. Ibid., 22.

11. Ibid.

12. Ibid., 18.

13. Ibid., 165.

14. Ibid., 171.

15. Ibid., 192.

16. Ibid., 208.

17. Ibid., 54.

18. Ibid., 59.

19. Ibid., 208–09.

20. Ibid., 59.

21. Ibid., 10.

22. Ibid., 8.

23. Ibid., 717.

24. Ibid., 608.

25. Ibid., 609.

26. Ibid., 610.

27. Ibid., Chapters 17–18: "Dilemmas I and II."

28. What follows has been adapted from my "Faith as a Way of Knowing in John of the Cross and Edith Stein," in Martin Boler and Anthony Cernera, eds., *The Contribution of Monastic Life to the Church and the World* (Fairfield, CT: Sacred Heart University Press, 2006), 167–79.

29. Edith Stein, *Science of the Cross*, trans. Hilda Graef (Chicago: Regnery, 1960), xxi.

30. Edith Stein, *Endliches und Ewiges Sein*, (Leuven: Nauwelaerts, 1950; Freiburg: Herder, 1950), viii.

31. Edith Stein, *Self-Portrait in Letters, 1916–1942*, trans. Josephine Koeppel, OCD (Washington, DC: Institute of Carmelite Studies, 1993), #29a.

32. Ibid., #149.

33. Ibid., #102.

34. Ibid., #103.

35. Ibid., #93a.

36. Ibid., #31.

37. Ibid., #32.

38. Ibid., #100.

39. Ibid., #158a.

40. Ibid., #45.

41. Saint John of the Cross, *Ascent of Mount Carmel* (Collected Works, trans. K. Kavanaugh and O. Rodriguez (Washington D.C.: Institute of Carmelite Studies, 1979), 2.5.3.

42. Ibid., 2.9.1.

43. Ibid., 2.5.3.

44. Ibid.

45. Aquinas, *Summa Theologiae*, I, 12, 13, 3.

46. Ibid.

47. Ibid., II, 2, 4, 5.

48. Saint John of the Cross, *Ascent of Mount Carmel*, 2.8.4.

49. Ibid., 2.8.1.

50. Saint Thomas Aquinas, *Summa Theologiae*, II, 2, 4, 5.

51. Saint John of the Cross, *Ascent of Mount Carmel*, 2.6.1.

52. Saint John of the Cross, *The Living Flame of Love* (*Collected Works*, trans. K. Kavanaugh and O. Rodriguez (Washington D.C.: Institute of Carmelite Studies, 1979), 1.1.

53. Ibid., 1.3–4.

54. Edith Stein, *Endliches und Ewiges Sein*, 320–21.

55. Ibid., 323–24.

INDEX